Praise

"Lisa Tenzin-Dolma has made an important in the field of archetypal astrology. Woven with mythic lore, astronomy and more, this book illuminates the quest for self-knowledge through the archetypal stories we play out throughout our lives. Learn how to balance the gods and goddesses within to better understand your own natal chart through a mythic lens."

—DANIELLE BLACKWOOD, author of *The Twelve Faces of the Goddess* and *A Lantern in the Dark*

"This book is a valuable resource for anyone who wants to take their understanding of astrology to the next level, as well as for anyone that loves myth and magical storytelling. *Stories in the Stars* is a fresh and enlightening approach to interpreting horoscopes and understanding the role myth and the archetypes of classical deities plays in our natal charts. This is a book you will refer to again and again."

—DODIE GRAHAM MCKAY, author of *Earth Magic* and *A Witch's Ally*

"*Stories in the Stars* is another stellar contribution you won't want to miss if you love history, stories, and astrology. Lisa has taken ancient culture mythology and aligned the planets and asteroids with the mythological heroes and heroines, giving new meaning to our natal charts and readings.... I found her insights to be fascinating and her associations mind-shifting. This is a brand-new landscape of understating natal charts and explaining our unique traits, strengths, and weaknesses through mythological personalities. Treat yourself to this book and learn how you fit into the realm of myths and planetary significance...I promise you will come away with valuable insights, a deeper understanding of yourself, and a boatload of entertaining stories from the pantheon."

—KAC YOUNG, PhD, ND, CMRM, author of *Crystal Power*

Stories
in the Stars

To Write to the Author

If you wish to contact the author or would like more information about this book, please write to the author in care of Llewellyn Worldwide Ltd. and we will forward your request. Both the author and publisher appreciate hearing from you and learning of your enjoyment of this book and how it has helped you. Llewellyn Worldwide Ltd. cannot guarantee that every letter written to the author can be answered, but all will be forwarded. Please write to:

Lisa Tenzin-Dolma
℅ Llewellyn Worldwide
2143 Wooddale Drive
Woodbury, MN 55125-2989
Please enclose a self-addressed stamped envelope for reply,
or $1.00 to cover costs. If outside the U.S.A., enclose
an international postal reply coupon.

Many of Llewellyn's authors have websites with additional information and resources. For more information, please visit our website at http://www.llewellyn.com.

Stories
in the Stars

Greek Myths & Deities within Western Astrology

Lisa Tenzin-Dolma

LLEWELLYN
WOODBURY, MINNESOTA

First Edition published in 2005 as *Understanding Planetary Myths* by Quantum, an
imprint of W. Foulsham & Co.Ltd.

SECOND EDITION
First Printing, 2025

Book design by Rordan Brasington
Cover art by Helena Elias
Cover design by Verlynda Pinckney
Editing by Laura Kurtz

Llewellyn Publications is a registered trademark of Llewellyn Worldwide Ltd.

Library of Congress Cataloging-in-Publication Data (Pending)
ISBN: 978-0-7387-8066-5

Llewellyn Publications
A Division of Llewellyn Worldwide Ltd.
2143 Wooddale Drive
Woodbury, MN 55125-2989
www.llewellyn.com

Printed in the United States of America

© Amber Tenzin-Dolma

About the Author

Lisa Tenzin-Dolma has been fascinated by stories and symbolism since her nomadic childhood in the UK, Malta, Malaysia, and Singapore, as well as through travel to Greece in her twenties followed by several years living in the Irish Republic. Her passion for reading led her to the mythological stories from world cultures from the age of eight, and she realized early on that the characters in the myths—especially ancient Greek and Roman myths—struck sympathetic chords with specific areas of the psyche that went on to reflect outwardly through attitudes and life experiences. Her curiosity about the workings of the mind led her to the study of astrology in 1979, when her eldest son was born. Through studying it, she discovered an interest in the powerful resonances between the planets and their myths that she developed over the years. This included the study of astrological psychology with the late Bruno and Louise Huber, who founded the Astrological Psychology Institute in Zurich in 1968, and whose methods were developed in collaboration with Roberto Assagioli, the founder of psychosynthesis. The Huber method focuses on astrology as a form of psychology that offers insights into the individual's inner mind and life, exploring potential that can be accessed and developed.

Author of thirty-four published books, her thirty-one nonfiction books delve into a wide range of self-help subjects; she has also published three novels. She lives in Bath, England.

Acknowledgments

Writing a book is similar to giving birth to a child. There is the conception of the idea, the inner absorption as it takes shape within you, the transition between the mysterious beauty of the blank pages of possibility, and the emergence of the child born of thought; the solid reality as it takes form in its entirety. Many people (too many to mention here) are involved during the gestation period, the time before it is handed over to those who will clothe it and speed its way into the wider world.

Dodie Graham McKay, my friend and fellow author, is the main reason that this book is now in your hands. She had a copy of the out-of-print first edition of this book and suggested that Llewellyn may be interested in it. I was excited about the idea, so Dodie passed on her copy to her editor, who was enthusiastic and passed it on to Acquisitions editor Amy Glaser—and, thanks to Amy and her team, here it is in its updated form. Huge thanks to all of you and to everyone at Llewellyn! Author and friend Kac Young has been my cheerleader and an inspirational force for around twenty years, and we co-wrote *The "Supposedly" Enlightened Person's Guide to Raising a Dog*, which was a bundle of fun to work together on. Thank you, Kac!

For sustenance on all levels I have my family to thank, especially my late parents, my sister, and my five children. My parents planted many seeds during my early years by showing me that each country we lived in was our home, by firing my curiosity, and by encouraging me to become immersed in many different cultures and their philosophies. My children soaked up tales of myths from many cultures before and after this book was conceived, asking questions that led me to fresh views of the scenery of the mind and imagination.

Acknowledgments

Friends provided (and still do) emotional nourishment and stimulating discussion. Loving thanks to all of them, especially Carole Cox, Yolanda Scott, Virginie Guilbot, Annie Rawlings, Paul Lipscombe, Michael Eastwood, Marius Von Brasch, Marcus and Liz Blosch, and Paul Halpern.

And last but certainly not least, I acknowledge my debt to the Greek poet Homer, whose *Odyssey* and *Iliad*, read and absorbed in my childhood, sparked the ideas that led me along the pathways of the mind and provided the foundation for my fascination with mythology. I would also like to acknowledge the tremendous inspiration and enthusiasm of the late, great Bruno and Louise Huber, who helped open the portal into a new way of interpreting natal charts.

Contents

Introduction

We humans are complex beings, capable of tapping into our vast innate potential to discover and express the very best of ourselves. At some point we all ask ourselves these two intriguing questions: "Who am I?" "How can I live my best, most fulfilling life?" Archetypal astrology can enhance your natal chart readings and help direct you to the answers.

The study of astrology is intended to foster a sense of self-empowerment and self-understanding. Your natal chart gives indications of how you can develop your potential to its fullest. It shows character traits, attitudes, gifts, and weaknesses. These can all be worked with even more constructively when you include an understanding of the ancient Greek and Roman archetypes whom the planets and asteroids are named after.

If you view the planets and asteroids and their corresponding deities' stories as aspects of yourself, you'll be able to discover which ones you express most fluently and which are repressed, denied, or ignored. The crux of any system of self-understanding, astrology included, is striving toward wholeness, the full integration and acceptance of yourself. Gifts can be developed and challenges

1

overcome, viewed as tools that help you develop compassion and strength of character.

The ancient deities upon which archetypal astrology is based can be viewed as musical notes in the symphony of the mind. Each note is heard as a voice within the psyche that we tune in to, depending on our focus. Some are loud and clear, others form background music. When combined by way of aspects between the planets (that is, their relationships with each other), some are harmonious, whereas others create discord. Each has its own voice and will speak out at some point, even if that voice is quieter than the others. The positions of the planets and asteroids in your birth chart reveal which archetypes speak loudest within you and which whisper softly. Because all of these can be understood as aspects of ourselves, we can decide whether a voice can be coaxed into making itself heard more clearly or instead choose to soften the one that dominates too frequently. We can write a new musical score for our lives through arranging the notes in the way that best suits our purposes.

We are, in essence, more than merely the sum of the planetary influences that prevailed at the moment of birth—our innate potential is vast. Yet understanding those influences can greatly enrich us, showing us how and why we act and react in certain ways. Unhealthy patterns can be broken, new possibilities can be explored, and our lives can become richer.

Let us look at the notes in this symphony more closely. Once you listen to them individually, you can discover their places in your own psyche and see how their vibrant notes add to the verses and choruses of your own psychological song.

Part 1
The Planets

Around 4.6 billion years ago, gravitational forces drew a giant cloud of interstellar gas and dust inward, where it began to collapse into itself. As it contracted, the combined forces of gravity and increased density made this new solar nebula spin faster and faster until it looked rather like a child's spinning top in a cosmic playground. The dense matter clumped together and birthed our sun, the planets, and asteroids, each held in place by the sun's gravitational pull.

The planets took on their own defining qualities according to their distance from the sun and their individual orbits. Like dewdrops in a sensitive web of vibrating strands, the sun and planets each exerted their influence over the others from the beginning, exchanging resonances that affected the growth and development of all. Some effects were subtle, others more noticeable. As its orbit moved closer to the sun, Jupiter's gravitational pull caused sunspots that affected weather systems on Earth. The moon influenced Earth's tides. Debris from comets and asteroids that passed too close or from the deaths of embryonic planets left scars on planetary surfaces and shifted orbits into different courses.

When humans appeared on Earth, they looked at the skies and saw patterns in the lights that each held stories and secrets. Curiosity led our distant ancestors to decipher these patterns; the symbols in the sky came to reflect stories and symbols that emerged through the human psyche. And within the larger patterns of the constellations were lights that moved and could be tracked: the wanderers, the planets.

It became apparent that these wanderers also carved out their own trails through the skies; if observed carefully, these paths could charter predictable courses. Some, like Mercury, moved swiftly. Others, the outer planets, moved slowly, taking years to traverse an area of sky. The ancients found that different configurations brought about particular influences. Astrology came into being.

Our need for story, the externalization of the imagination, forged links between the myths that formed a cultural backdrop and the bright planets that made pinpoints in the canopy of night stars. The planets (and later the asteroids) were named after deities, and their astrological interpretations were based on the personalities of these gods and goddesses. Even in modern times this still holds true. Through a blend of observational science, mysticism, and intuition, the ancients observed connections forged as strongly as the gravitational forces that brought our solar system from a nebulous, gaseous state into a group of planets circling a star on an arm of the Milky Way galaxy.

Chapter One

In the Beginning

The Olympian gods and goddesses whose stories are linked so powerfully to our solar system were not the first rulers in the mythology of ancient Greece. The tale begins with Chaos, the state of flux from which all forms emerge. In modern times as in the distant past, where memory, dreams, and imagination created and destroyed worlds, Chaos lends its name to the maelstrom within which all possibilities arise. In the science of chaos theory, within that matrix of constantly shifting energy is found a plethora of what could be considered miracles. The ancients were tuned in to this, and their myths reflect the contemporary perception of order arising out of disorder.

Floating on this sea of Chaos, the primeval state, was the Egg of Night. From this cosmic egg, symbol of the seed of creation, emerged Eros, the primal force and the embodiment of the principle of love. He used his arrows and torch to pierce through to the forms beneath and illuminate them. Through Eros, a new world came into being.

The earth goddess, Gaia, arose and provided a home for the deities of the future. She birthed Ouranos, the sky god, who became her consort. Then came the mountains, nymphs, and the sea. The realm of the gods encompassed sky, earth, and sea, night and day, darkness and light. The union of Gaia and Ouranos brought forth the titans: Oceanus, Hyperion, Iapetus, Theia, Rhea, Themis, Mnemosyne, Phoebe, Tethys, and Kronos.

However, the survival of these primal deities appeared at first to be uncertain. Fearful that a child of his would usurp him, Ouranos imprisoned each newborn within Gaia's body to prevent their emergence from the earth. Understandably unhappy about the situation, Gaia devised a plan. When Kronos was born, she hid him in her depths and gave him a sickle made of sharp stone. The infant lay in wait, and when Ouranos came to mate with Gaia, Kronos leaped out, severed his father's genitals and threw them into the sea. The foam that rose from this birthed Aphrodite, the goddess of love and beauty. Stray drops of blood became the Erinyes, the Furies. Kronos released his siblings from the prison of their mother's body, and the titans took power.

Kronos married his sister, Rhea, and their union brought forth Hestia, Demeter, Hera, Hades, Poseidon, and Zeus but he swallowed each as they were born. In desperation, Rhea turned to her parents for help during her pregnancy with Zeus. Gaia and Ouranos told her to go to Crete, so she fled there to give birth. She hid the infant in a cave and gave Kronos a boulder wrapped in swaddling clothes, that he swallowed immediately, thinking it was Zeus. Cared for in secret by his mother, Zeus grew strong enough to overthrow his father and force him to regurgitate the others. The stone that Kronos had mistaken for Zeus was placed at Delphi, the womb of the earth. The new generation of gods, the Olympians, then took center stage.

Ancient Greece

The topography of the ancient Greek understanding of the world was based on their belief that it was flat and circular, and that their country was set in the center of this disc with Mount Olympus, the home of the gods who held power over the affairs of humankind, overshadowing them. The earth's disc was divided into two by the Mediterranean, which the Greeks called "the Sea." Surrounding their Earth was the "River Ocean" that fed the central sea.

The Greeks' flat, circular Earth was subdivided according to the four directions. In the north dwelt the Hyperboreans. This land was inaccessible, and its inhabitants were said to live in a state of bliss, untrammeled by old age, disease, or war. Later, Apollo, the sun god, would travel there each year for sanctuary.

In the east was the realm of the dawn and the sun, moon, and stars. These rose from the eastern aspect of the ocean surrounding Earth to travel across the sky, bringing light to the lives of both gods and mortals.

The south was inhabited by the Aethiopians, who lived in a similar state of peace and harmony to the Hyperboreans. These people were so favored by the Olympians that the gods and goddesses would visit them and share in their feasts.

To the west lay the Elysian Plain, also called the "Fortunate Fields" and "the Isles of the Blessed." This was the place where mortals who had the gods' favor were taken to receive the gift of immortality.

Mount Olympus overlooked Earth. Near its peak was a gateway of clouds that were guarded by the Seasons, who allowed safe passage to the gods and goddesses who had their home there.

When Kronos (Saturn) overthrew his father and ended the rule of the titans, the new generation of Olympians began: Zeus

(Jupiter), Demeter (Ceres), Hera (Juno), Hades (Pluto), Poseidon (Neptune), and Hestia (Vesta). Later, Zeus fathered the next generation of Olympians, and the die was cast for myths that have endured over millennia.

Among these celestial beings were many others whose relevance is still felt. These include the nine Muses, who inspired poetry and song; the three Graces, who presided over all celebrations; the three Fates, who spun the threads of human destiny and cut these threads at the end of life; and the three Furies, who wreaked vengeance when justice had not been served.

Each deity had a role to play both in celestial and mortal affairs. Their mythical lives still inhabit the deep realms of the human mind. To the ancient Greeks, the gods ruled from above and below—from the heavens, sea, and underworld. In modern times, their voices speak to us from within, sparked by our personal astrological connections and configurations as well as through our resonance with aspects of our personalities to which we most strongly relate. The old gods are not forgotten—their influence still touches us, and we can learn much from them.

Chapter Two

The Sun—Apollo

Apollo rules the Sun, Leo, and the fifth house.

The archetype of the sun god is expressed through the essential symbolism of Apollo as the favorite son of Zeus/Jupiter, ruler of the Olympians. As the one chosen to embody leadership qualities and the son to whom the mantle of succession to the throne was pinned, Apollo was trained from an early age to assume power and view it as his birthright.

As the central focus of the solar system, the creative and generative force with equal power to give and take life, the sun holds a unique position. Apollo reflects this through his archetypal resonance. Like the sun, he stands alone, set apart from his clan by the role bequeathed upon him by his father. His extrovert qualities are enhanced through his annual retreat to Hyperborea, a place where none can follow him. His nature is to shine his light on all while holding silently to the mystery of his inner self.

The Birth of Apollo

Apollo was born on Delos, a barren Greek island, after a difficult nine-day labor. His mother, Leto, was a titan, one of the forerunners of the Olympian gods, and she conceived Apollo and his twin sister, Artemis, after Zeus seduced her. Zeus was notorious for his affairs, even though the jealousy of his long-suffering wife Hera was legendary; frequently, she would commit vengeful acts of retribution toward her husband's lovers. When Hera heard of the affair between him and Leto, she made it clear that anyone who helped Leto would be punished. Alone and afraid, Leto therefore wandered the earth in search of a sanctuary where she could bring her children into the world. Eventually, in the final stages of labor, she arrived at what would later be named Delos, where she gave birth to Artemis, goddess of the moon, the hunt, and childbirth.

Artemis helped with the arduous delivery of her brother, and Apollo was eventually born beneath a palm tree on the seventh day of the month. As he was being born, swans circled the island seven times, giving voice in celebration.

Exhausted from the trials she had endured, Leto handed Apollo over into the safekeeping of Themis, another pre-Olympian goddess, who nurtured him and raised him on nectar and ambrosia, the food of the gods. She passed on her rulership of the art of prophecy to Apollo and groomed him for a leadership role within the Olympian pantheon. Apollo's golden beauty, keen intellect, and confident masculinity endeared him to Zeus, who gave him a chariot pulled by swans and appointed him as his favorite son. Apollo rode this chariot to draw him on his daily journey across the sky, and it was also the vehicle that would take him in the future to the mystical realm of the Hyperboreans, a place in the north of Greece associated with the Pleiades constellation.

Personality Traits

Apollo was intensely inquisitive with a tremendous thirst for knowledge. His keen intellect and abundant self-confidence made him the center of attention, particularly where his father was concerned, which coincided with his planetary position as the brightest light in the sky. Though somewhat detached and aloof, he was cheerful and sunny natured, having the conviction that logic ruled supreme over emotion.

Yet Apollo was also extremely competitive. To come first and always be the best was the driving force behind his impulses and achievements. His methods were not always laudable, though they always seemed fair to his mind. Apollo was a thinker who refused to allow his emotions to take precedence. Although revered and respected for his mental clarity, his skill in archery, and his power over the making and upholding of law and order, he needed time away from Olympia. He spent a year in retreat in Hyperborea and afterward went there for three months each winter to replenish himself and allow the connection with his spiritual nature to be strengthened. This time marks the days on Earth when the sun loses its warmth and does not nurture the land.

Apollo's ability to aim for a goal and never miss his mark reflects the unerring confidence of those who are ruled astrologically by the Sun. The awareness of the goal creates an awareness of the future—what can be sought and attained—tying to Apollo's rulership of prophecy. He had a deep-rooted need to win, a compulsion backed up by a calculating quality that viewed the means as necessary to any end result. Determination rather than emotion drove him to attain his goals, and his ability for careful planning gave him a long-range view. Apollo embodies the striving for success and recognition.

Prophecy

The oracle at Delphi was situated at the base of Mount Parnassus. Delphi was considered the womb of the world, and its inner chamber was called the Omphalos, "navel." Beneath this mysterious space in the womb of the earth, where clefts opened from deep within and gases mingled with the herbs burned to aid the oracle to access altered states of awareness, lived the Python, a great snake born from Gaia. The Python whispered to Pythia, the oracular priestess, who then intoned the information she had received. This was a feminine realm, embodying intuition, mystery of the unknown, and the emergence of the knowledge of deep self into the light of consciousness. Apollo's logic could not accept this and did not wish to. He sought control over the mystery and placed his own version of prophecy in its stead.

One of Apollo's first acts was to use his golden bow and arrow to slay the Python. He put priestesses of his own in charge, who became known as Pythonesses, and their prophecies were interpreted by Apollo's priests, thus ensuring that control of this previously female domain was handed over to men. Gaia was outraged by the murder of her child and went to Zeus, calling for retribution. To appease her, Zeus insisted that Apollo became a slave to a mortal man for a period of time.

Apollo himself had no prophetic abilities, though the rulership of the oracle belonged to him and he could transfer the gifts of prophecy to others. People came to the oracle for help, advice, and purification. From this place, Apollo dispensed justice and made laws.

The innermost chamber at Delphi contained the grave of Dionysus, the god of wine and ecstasy. During the three months of each year when Apollo retreated to Hyperborea, Dionysus had charge of the temple. These half-siblings, both with Zeus as their father, were diametrically opposite in temperament. The nature of Dionysus was abandoned and wild, given to excess in drinking, dancing, and lovemaking. The contrast between Apollo's government of the oracle and that of Dionysus indicates that even when all efforts are made to suppress the wild self, it must re-emerge when the civilized self temporarily steps back.

Relationships

Apollo was not always lucky in love. His lovers were chosen for their beauty, intelligence, and independence, but he often sought out women who were his opposite in nature only to be rejected by them. His cool, logical impulses craved union with the fey, sensitive, psychic aspect of femininity that his detached, rational mind could not understand.

Several of his romances led to tragedy. His first love, for Daphne, a naiad and daughter of a river god, was unreciprocated and came about as a result of Apollo's arrogance. He had sneered at Eros, the god of love, insisting that Eros was a lesser man with a bow and arrow. In retribution, Eros shot a golden love-arrow into Apollo's heart, smiting him with yearning for Daphne. Into Daphne's heart he aimed a love-repelling arrow that made her flee from Apollo's ardent advances. When he pursued her, she cried to her father for help and was turned into a laurel tree just as Apollo reached her. Apollo made the tree one of his symbols and decorated his hair with wreaths made from the leaves. Today, the laurel wreath symbolizes victory and leadership.

Another pursued by Apollo was Cassandra, the daughter of Priam and Hecuba, the king and queen of Troy. Apollo fell in love with Cassandra, and, although she did not love him in return, she longed for the gift of prophecy and so agreed to become Apollo's lover in exchange. After he bestowed the gift on her, she refused to keep her side of the bargain. Furious, Apollo ensured that no one would believe her when she spoke of the future, and Cassandra was shut away by her own kind, considered insane and unwilling to listen to her.

In relationships, Apollo was mostly cool and detached, choosing strong women who would provide a challenge. But he insisted on being both the center of attention and the one holding the balance of power. His preoccupation with order and his need to retreat for three months each year made for an emotional distance that was not easy to have in relationships.

Apollo had three children. Asclepius was the son of Apollo and Coronis. A raven appointed by Apollo to watch over Coronis through her pregnancy told Apollo that she had been unfaithful to him. He killed her in a rage, then as her body was placed on the funeral pyre, he regretted his hasty action and rescued Asclepius from her womb. The boy was reared by the centaur Chiron, the healer and tutor to the gods, and Asclepius in turn became the god of healing and medicine. His powers were so great that he could even bring the dead to life. This led to his downfall when Hades, god of the underworld where the shades (souls) of the dead were taken, complained that his realm was in danger of becoming obsolete because of Asclepius' gift. Zeus agreed with Hades that this would not do and killed Asclepius with a thunderbolt. Apollo insisted that his son be set in the heavens as Ophiuchus, the serpent-bearer, so that he could still watch over Earth.

Another of Apollo's sons was Aristaeus, who was born through a union with the nymph, Cyrene, and was also brought up by Chiron. He became a healer and visionary and was the protector of flocks and agriculture.

Orpheus was Apollo's son by his liaison with the muse Calliope. Apollo gave Orpheus a lyre and taught him to play it so beautifully that none could resist the music. He fell in love with Eurydice, a nymph, and they were married, but she died from a snakebite and was taken to the underworld realm of Hades. Distraught with grief, Orpheus made his way down to the underworld, knowing that few who went there could return. He calmed the ferryman who took the souls of the dead across the River Styx and sang the fierce three-headed dog, Cerberus, to sleep in order to gain access to Hades's domain. Once inside, Orpheus pleaded with Hades and his wife, Persephone, to give him back his beloved wife. They agreed to release her, providing Orpheus did not attempt to look at her until they were back in the realm of the living. However, he was so desperate to see her that before they reached the surface, he looked back to check that she was following him and lost her forever.

Each of Apollo's sons, though tragic, were gifted, suggesting the sun's tremendous creative and generative power.

Sibling Rivalry

Although the relationship between Apollo and Artemis was close, they enjoyed pitting their formidable wits against each other. Both were superlative archers, and Apollo jealously plotted to get rid of his sister's lover, Orion, through capitalizing on her competitive streak. After secretly watching Orion swim far out to sea, Apollo challenged her to shoot one of her silver arrows at a distant dot on the ocean. Artemis did so, only to discover afterward that she had killed her lover. Distraught, she placed him in the sky as the constellation Orion, accompanied by Sirius, one of her dogs.

Hermes, Apollo's younger half-brother, was the son of Zeus and Maia, whose titan father, Atlas, carried the world on his shoulders. On the day that Hermes was born, he invented the lyre and then stole some prized cattle from Apollo. Disguising his footsteps with branches, he drove fifty of Apollo's cattle backward, thinking his trick would not be discovered. Apollo, however, saw through the ploy and confronted Hermes, who by then had roasted and eaten two cows and was pretending to be asleep in his mother's cave. Although Hermes at first denied any involvement, eventually he agreed to exchange his lyre for the stolen cattle and was allowed to keep the remaining forty-eight cows.

Apollo's music followed the laws of harmony and logic; the wild abandon of gods such as Dionysus was not for him. Apollo's music was ordered and clear, and the relationship between music and mathematics is very Apollonian. He strove to create sounds that calmed the heart and soothed wilder emotions in songs that evoked a sense of purity of spirit.

Archetypal Resonance

Apollo as an archetype embodies the ability to see clearly and understand what is seen. His gaze is far-reaching and all-encompassing. He is the arrow that drives straight to the heart of the goal. He is the maker and upholder of laws. The overview is more important to him than the details—he looks at how the whole will be affected rather than its components.

The Apollo archetype is the master of control, logical thought processes, and clear, concise assessment and judgement. Thinking is more important than feeling. The mind rules over the emotions, though he is susceptible to flattery due to his sense of pride. Along with order and harmony, knowledge is his primary concern because it brings about understanding, growth, and expansion. As Zeus's favorite son, he embodies the need and expectation to shine among the company of others. When this element of Apollo's nature is fulfilled, the archetype truly comes into its own and displays a benevolence experienced as a warm glow that radiates far beyond the immediate sphere.

The Astronomy of the Sun

The sun, a young star in its prime, shines high above us, unaffected by our human viewpoints and considerations. Born around 4.6 billion years ago from a swirling molecular cloud of gases and expected to survive in its present state for at least a further five billion years, the sun is fueled by nuclear energy generated deep within its core. There is no solid rock on the sun—it is gaseous from the surface to the core. The light that emanates from its surface only gives clues as to the inner temperatures and is strong enough to illuminate the far reaches of the solar system.

As the center of our solar system and our source of life, the sun casts light on Earth, vivifies, reveals, and defines the shapes and forms that it illuminates. The areas where the sun shines brightest contain the deepest shadows as contrasts are picked out and clarified.

The sun symbolizes knowledge, birth, growth, creativity, order, logic, and spiritual illumination. Nothing can be hidden from the sun's eye; it sees all and ultimately judges nothing. The sun warms Earth and facilitates growth, but too much exposure to it burns fertile earth to a wasteland and creates barrenness. It engenders respect. In the winter, the sun's strength wanes, as Apollo retires to the temporary sanctuary of Hyperborea to gather his energy for the months to come.

In Your Natal Chart

Apollo is a ruling influence in your natal chart, just as he is a powerful force on Olympus. The Sun sign you are born under provides the lens for your self-expression and shows how you develop and manifest your creative impulses. Astrologically, the Sun represents the core of your being, your true inner nature. Even if other archetypal voices may appear to speak more loudly through your natal chart, the Sun's position reveals how you experience and express your inner sense of purpose and self-empowerment and indicates the areas in which you shine.

The Sun rules growth, clear-sightedness, logic, and spiritual as well as temporal understanding. It gives clues as to areas of achievement, attainment and success, and reveals the focus of the inner drive that can be directed toward your goals in life. Confidence, passion, and the need to be recognized and acknowledged by others are all denoted by the position of the sun in your natal chart. There is a sense of immediacy in the area of your chart in which the sun is situated, and this is manifested through its position in the astrological sign and the house it occupies. The Sun insists on expressing itself; even when hidden behind a cloud, its influence is felt.

Aspects to the Sun take these insights of expression further and reveal the relationships between the different archetypal forces that resonate within you. The aspects also indicate whether the positive or challenging qualities of those archetypes are being brought into play and give a clearer perspective on how best to work with them.

If you are expressing Apollonian qualities to the detriment of other areas of the self (if your thinking is predominant over feeling), Apollo is ruling you rather than being just one element of the psyche. Where the Sun is concerned, knowing this can help you to gauge which qualities of Apollo are ruling you rather than being ruled by you. Depending on the Sun's position, the power principle that the Sun governs may be obvious and outwardly dynamic in your natal chart or lie deeper beneath the surface.

Apollo's influence is felt through your need to have a goal, an aim. The bow and arrow of Apollo's intent must have a target, otherwise it can turn against itself and be expressed as self-destructive impulses. Apollo's ability to see clearly and set aside any emotional considerations in favor of logic, reason, and forethought casts light on areas that may be missed or ignored if emotions are running high. Your powers of judgment are gifts Apollo has bestowed upon you, gifts that stem from an inner urge toward rightness and morality.

There is a competitive element in the Sun derived from Apollo's need and desire to always be first; to be the favored child, the sought-after lover, the voice of reason, the fount of knowledge. The Sun, like Apollo, must be the brightest luminary in the sky.

Rulership of the Sun

The Sun governs Leo. Leos are gregarious; generous with their resources whether it is time, energy, money, or affection; creative; and magnanimous, especially when others are around to notice. The symbol for Leo, the lion, has a mane similar to the rays of the sun and is known as the king of beasts. Statues of Apollo are easily recognized due to his beautiful physique and halo of curly hair, reminiscent of the sun's rays.

The qualities of Apollo are at their most pronounced in Leos. His role as the favorite son is often played out through this sign, as Leos thrive on praise and actively seek it out. Apollo's skill and determination are apparent in the Sun's rulership of Leo, as is his ability to be the one in power who delegates with flair and aplomb. Apollo as patron of the oracle at Delphi did not need the actual skills of prophecy. His charisma was such that others would carry out tasks for him while he accepted the approbation.

Apollo's annual retreat to the sanctuary of Hyperborea is reflected in the Leonine love of sunshine and a place to stretch out catlike and relax. The retreat also satisfies the need for a change in routine and provides the space for allowing an influx of creative ideas. The outgoing, active nature of the Sun expresses itself most positively when balanced by periods of leisure and the renewal of connection with the spiritual self.

When the Sun holds a prominent position in the natal chart or is strongly aspected to other planets through conjunctions, squares, or oppositions, issues connected with the will, desire, or ego can dominate. Apollo was compelled to always be first and best, a drive evident in his roles as the favorite and the brightest luminary in the sky. There can be a tendency to dominate because of this that can be tempered through finding positive outlets for expression that naturally result in praise and respect from others. Positive aspects indicate that the will is used for the benefit of others as well as the self, and Apollo's sharp intelligence and focus can be directed into extraordinary creativity and benevolence.

The Apollonian sense of drama is apparent in strong Sun aspects; potentially resulting in abundant creativity and talented acting and role-playing. The charisma is so strong that others will gravitate to it, hoping to become part of a charmed circle in which the Sun is center. Apollo liked being center stage even in his relationships with his siblings, and he reveled in creating scenes that would gather him praise and renown.

The sun's warmth draws us in, yet its benevolence hides a certain detachment. It shines on all regardless of status or circumstance and is close to few; it is set apart from others by its very nature. Attempt to move too close and you could be burned. Respect it and you will grow and flourish in its light.

Chapter Three

The Moon — Artemis / Diana

Artemis rules the Moon, Cancer, and the fourth house.

The archetype of the virgin goddess defines the essential qualities of Artemis. Contrary to the modern perception of a virgin as one who is not sexually awakened, the true meaning of this term refers to something untouched and complete within itself. Along with Athena and Hestia, Artemis retains her own secret, mysterious aspects. She is aware of her own innate sense of wholeness and does not seek approbation from others. She is true to her own instincts, drives, and desires. Artemis follows her own course and accepts the consequences of her decisions and actions.

Because of this inner integrity, the virgin goddess archetype has an inward-looking focus and an ability to recognize motives and act on them, regardless of whether these make sense to other people. Artemis goes her own way. She seeks out the solitude that enables her to feel connected to the natural world, and that enables her to define herself in her own eyes and not through the eyes of others. She is self-sufficient, self-contained, and self-assured.

The Birth of Artemis

Twin sister to Apollo and the firstborn, Artemis immediately supported her mother, Leto, during her brother's long and arduous birth. This earned her the roles of goddess of childbirth and of the moon, the planet that was once believed to strongly influence women's menstrual cycles. Whereas Apollo was given over to the care of Themis, Artemis stayed with her mother and took on a protective role. When she was brought before Zeus, her father and the king of the gods, he was so impressed by her that he offered her any gift that she wished for. Artemis chose a silver bow and arrows (the metal associated with the moon), a pack of hounds, and a band of nymphs who would live in the wilderness with her. Her requests were granted.

Artemis the Protectress

Artemis is the protector of women, particularly during childbirth, and she always answered pleas for help with swift (sometimes merciless) action. She rescued her mother from an attempted rape by a giant, Tityus, and killed him. When the queen Niobe slighted Leto, Artemis and Apollo took their revenge by hunting down and killing Niobe's children; Artemis killing her six daughters, and Apollo her six sons, before turning Niobe into a pillar of stone.

The dark side of the moon, the private side that never turns its face to the light of the sun and the eyes of those on Earth, is also Artemis's domain. She loved the dark and would hunt by moonlight and the light of torches. No man was allowed to spy on her or her nymphs, and any who attempted to do so were met with immediate punishment. When the hunter Actaeon stumbles across Artemis and her nymphs bathing and could not resist watching, Artemis turned him into a stag, whereupon he was pursued and brought down by his own dogs.

Artemis and her nymphs formed a sisterhood echoed in modern times whenever women come together with a common aim whether at leisure or in protest. This mutual support is beneficial to all and is encompassing and protective. The underlying purpose is self-empowerment and self-exploration in the open and accepting company of other women. Men are excluded from this Artemisian domain though not from the outward lives of the goddess or the women who seek to embody aspects of her. This sense of female community acts as a foundation for the outer lives of relationships and work. The urge to walk in moonlight and starlight, to be alone in the countryside and woods, to bathe in a stream or pool unobserved all spring from the Artemisian qualities deep within us.

Relationships

Orion, a mortal hunter, was Artemis's great love. There are several versions of the Artemis-Orion myth; the one that appears here is the version described by Jean Shinoda Bolen, MD, in her book *Goddesses in Everywoman*, in which Artemis unknowingly killed Orion as a result of Apollo's jealousy. Angry that his sister's affection was directed toward another man, Apollo watched Orion swim out to sea and plotted his revenge. When Orion was nothing but a distant speck on the horizon, Apollo sought out Artemis and challenged her to hit the tiny dark shape floating far away in the distance. Unable to resist an opportunity to show off her archery prowess, Artemis aimed true and Orion was killed. When she discovered that she had been tricked and her lover was dead, she mourned Orion deeply and set him in the sky as the constellation, accompanied by her faithful hound, Sirius.

Artemis's love of solitude, her desire to be among a select band of trusted women, and her role as protector of women in need (whose pleas for help came through their associations with men) took precedence over romantic relationships. Indeed, men were in awe of or even afraid of her. Her strength, skill, and confidence could be intimidating to men, especially those who felt emasculated by women who were whole unto themselves and needed nothing from others. The nature of the moon reflects this—it is a partner of the sun, a friend of the dark, cool and detached while also capable of bringing the emotions of others to the surface.

Archetypal Resonance

Artemis as an archetype embodies the independent free thinker. She is determined to do things her way and finds all she needs within herself. Relationships are of secondary importance, as they draw her attention outward rather than inward, distracting her from her own goals and primary considerations.

Artemis embodies the ability to be fully focused. Nothing can distract her once a decision has been made. The Artemis archetype revels in competition because it spurs motivational impulses and creates longed-for challenge. There is a sense of community with other women, a singularity of vision and purpose, and an attunement to the realms of the hidden and mysterious.

The call of the wilderness is especially strong within the Artemis archetype, a symbol of the need to experience and navigate uncharted domains within ourselves, those hidden, often dark and rocky aspects of our inner nature. The wilderness is where the deep self resides; it is the wild, untamed self expressed through instinct and intuition that leads us to hidden truths.

The Astronomy of the Moon

The moon is estimated to be almost as old as our solar system, indicating that it was formed in the early stages of the planetary formations. Analysis showed that moon rocks from the lunar crust brought back from the Apollo XVI mission were estimated to be around 4.36 billion years old.

The moon's surface is scarred by meteorites, and its terrain consists of vast plains and mountain ranges. Its atmosphere has long since evaporated, but in the darkest areas where sunlight cannot reach are pools of water in the form of ice.

The rulership of the Moon by Artemis reveals the subtle, changeable, reflective side of this archetype. Moonlight casts very different shadows than sunlight. The Moon softly illuminates. Its glow draws our eyes and evokes deep emotions, whereas the sun is too bright to be looked at with the naked eye. Although the sun appears to dominate the moon, the new moon, the phase when Artemis is seen as being at her most powerful is when solar eclipses occur. The new moon passes between Earth and the sun, casting its shadow on the earth's surface and briefly blots out its sibling.

Our natural satellite, the moon is as important to the survival of life on Earth as the sun. The moon affects the ocean tides, the water in our cells and our blood, and our emotions. As it waxes and wanes, its changing face heightens the connection with the instinctual nature when it shows its fullest face, and gives its name to "lunacy"—the madness that comes through ploughing the depths of what is apparently hidden or forbidden.

Dreams are a gift of the moon, shining on us while we sleep, allowing access to the unconscious mind. And just as the moon appears to die each month only to be reborn and generate itself, so are the cells in our bodies repeatedly renewed in order to maintain health.

The cycles of the moon mirror the cycles of life: gestation, birth, growth, death, renewal. We see these cycles reflected in the plant and animal kingdoms in a continuous process of evolution. Creativity is an aspect of this evolution, the ability to connect with something deep within the self and give birth to new forms as a result. Lovers revere the moon, as do artists, poets, writers, and craftspeople because it is a continual reminder of the relationship we have with mystery.

In Your Natal Chart

The Moon in your natal chart governs the unconscious mind, deep emotions, instinct, and intuition. This planet rules your emotional responses and shows how early experiences colored your emotional outlook. The Moon's position reveals your relationship with your mother and with women in general. Depending upon the astrological sign and house it appears in, your imaginative visionary faculties and the ability to dream and to use your dreams for self-understanding are activated. The Moon's position also reveals issues of safety and security and whether your emotional needs are met.

Negative aspects to the Moon tend to show areas of your life where you experience a lack of comfort or security. Positive aspects indicate attunement to your emotional self and a high degree of intuition. The placement of the Moon indicates in which areas of your life you act out unconscious impulses and preconditioned responses and respond to stimuli, and it is also associated with memory. In essence, the Moon is the mirror of your feeling nature in your natal chart.

Just as Artemis is drawn to the wilderness, so does the influence of the Moon provide access to the secrets of the wild self; the inner aspect in which instinct, intuition, and deep connection with the natural world prevail. The Moon's inner drive is that of allowing change, of understanding that life moves in cycles, and the knowledge that the deep emotions can provide a powerful impetus for change if used constructively.

Although the sun appears initially to be more powerful than its bright twin, the two are equals; half of one whole that cannot be separated. The sun provides the energy for life, but its light makes growth and change possible when the moon reflects it. The feeling, intuitive, dreaming nature expressed through your Moon position underpins the outward expression of your personality found through your Sun sign.

Positive aspects between the Moon and other planets indicate a constructive ability to feel and express your emotions. They show how you connect to our inner nature and, through this, how you relate to others in an intuitive, compassionate manner. Negative aspects, depending on the planets and houses involved, can manifest as either repressed or suppressed emotions, tense relationships with women, the mother, or public figures, or a predisposition to be driven irrationally by the tides of feeling.

The Moon is the key to our memories and dreams, our fears, and our ability to plumb the hidden depths. The influence of Artemis as Moon goddess is felt through the desire to experience the female aspect of the self with power, strength, independence, and acceptance.

Rulership of the Moon

The Moon governs the astrological sign Cancer, whose symbol, the crab, lives out its life under the influences of the tides of the sea as the moon draws these across the earth. The sea embodies life through the emergence of the first creatures from the primeval soup eons ago. Symbolically, water signifies the emotions and the deep, hidden aspects of the psyche.

When the Moon is prominent in your natal chart, you are ruled by your emotional tides, even though you may prefer to hide your sensitivity beneath a tough exterior. Though strong, proud, and independent, Artemis cared deeply for those close to her and was fiercely protective by nature. She needed the company of her nymphs along with the attendant sense of community and belonging. But just like with her twin, Apollo, she also sought solitude, preferring wild places for renewal and replenishment. Although she could be merciless when her privacy was infringed upon, the company of kindred spirits was welcomed and celebrated if allowed a period of seclusion.

Children of the Moon are complex creatures, reluctant to be known too familiarly. They crave security and build strong, sometimes impenetrable defenses in order to hide their feelings of vulnerability. Like their archetype, they set their sights high, though they prefer to aim at what is attainable rather than take unnecessary risks. Competitiveness arises from the need to prove themselves and to hide their gentle sides, as they fear scorn more than anything. Like Artemis, they have a connection with the wild self and an urge to seek out places of solitude and safety.

In relationships, possessiveness can become an issue that can prove detrimental. In the story of Artemis and Orion, the goddess was tricked into killing her lover because of Apollo's jealousy that a mere mortal had all the attention that he felt should be his. When strongly felt in the natal chart, the Moon's influence can exert a powerful, all-encompassing pull on the emotions that can be difficult to deal with both for the loved one and for others.

When heard above the other elements in a person's psyche, the Artemis archetype is unwilling to compromise and refuses to listen to opinions that do not conform with their own. Yet there is an innate understanding of human nature and a profound sympathy and empathy for those in need of help.

The moon's glow is subtle, casting a cool, gentle radiance. This radiance allows that which is hidden to remain hidden; it does not pry or demand.

Chapter Four

Mercury—Hermes

Hermes/Mercury rules Mercury, Gemini, Virgo, and the third and sixth houses.

The essential quality of Hermes is communication. This god's fundamental aspects are the need to satisfy curiosity and the urge to forge links between others are. The dual nature of both the deity and the planet is reflected through the modes of communication expressed according to mood. Hermes embodies the exchange of ideas, the stimulation of the mind's quicksilver aspects that can occur through verbal and written interchange, a search for understanding, or even mischief-making designed to confuse others and provide Hermes with entertainment at their expense.

As an archetype, Hermes defines the epitome of adolescence with alternating boyish charm and hidden barbs, yet beneath it rests the urge to be of use. He is also the guide, the deity who alone has the skill to escort the souls of the dead from the light down to the underworld, the realm of Hades; to forge links between the conscious mind and the shadowy depths of the unconscious.

The Birth of Hermes

Hermes's mother, Maia, managed to escape Hera's vengeance, as Zeus seduced her while the latter was asleep. A daughter of Atlas, the titan who supported the world on his shoulders, Maia lived in the Pleiades constellation and was a quiet and retiring luminary.

Like other deities, Hermes sprang into action as soon as he left his mother's womb, immediately setting about making mischief. Within a few hours of birth, he invented the lyre using a tortoise shell as the body of the instrument to which he added strings. The music he made soothed and uplifted all who heard it. On the same day, intent on annoying his half-brother Apollo, he stole his prized cattle; when found out, Hermes was forced by an angry Zeus to hand over his lyre and the title of god of music to Apollo. His role as mischief-maker and trickster was set in place from birth, and he enjoyed creating havoc and playing tricks on his siblings.

In conflict, Hermes used cunning and guile rather than confrontation. He was a messenger for the gods and was called on by Zeus whenever his father needed someone or something retrieved and brought to him.

Personality Traits

Hermes was fun-loving, quick-thinking, and inventive. He could be immature and childlike, and his appearance was eternally youthful. However, he was also deceptive and manipulative, with no compunction about being creative with the truth. Truth, to Hermes, was easily twisted if that would bring about the results he desired. This trickster element in his nature made it possible for him to see through the machinations of others and find the kernel that always lay at the heart of the matter in order to turn situations to his advantage. Hermes was an opportunist, yet one who was always ready to take on the role of guide, both through the labyrinthine corridors of the mind and across physical terrain.

Hermes's winged sandals and helmet enabled him to travel swiftly and far, between the lofty heights of Mount Olympus to the earth and the underworld. His favored metal, quicksilver, reflects his fluid qualities and ability to shift instantly from one mode of thinking or physical place to another. This changeable aspect of his nature made him unpredictable and not always popular with members of his family, whose attitudes were more fixed. Hermes could not be pinned down. His approach was that of a shapeshifter, able to change form in an instant, though more in the mental sense than physical. He had a natural, easy charm that convinced those whom he had offended to forgive him after a cooling-off period.

The Messenger

Hermes's eloquence gave him a natural role as the god of speech and communication, earning him the title of messenger of the gods. He protected travelers, athletes, and thieves and was considered to bring good fortune to those he favored. A master wordsmith himself, he invented the alphabet and bequeathed the gift of writing to mortals, becoming a favorite of writers and public speakers.

As messenger, he interceded between gods and mortals, and he also acted as guide for those travelling to the underworld realm after death. He carried a caduceus, a staff entwined with two snakes and topped with wings, which denoted his position as herald of the gods and was used for resurrection as well as marking him as an individual of knowledge and authority. As an alchemical symbol, the caduceus represents the union of the masculine and feminine elements of the psyche; it also signifies death and rebirth, sexuality, and procreation through its similarity to the structure of

DNA in the body. Hermes is associated with magic and is often depicted as the Magician in the tarot.

Hermes could be kind and helpful, and came to the aid of Demeter and Persephone when Hades abducted Persephone and took her to the underworld to be his wife (the full story of Demeter and Persephone is told in chapter 13). When Persephone was released from the underworld, Hermes acted as her guide and took her back to a joyful reunion with her mother.

Relationships

Hermes had many liaisons and was reputed to be bisexual, but his mercurial nature meant that it was impossible for his lovers to pin him down and extract promises of commitment. His longest-lived affair was with Aphrodite. Their union brought forth a child, Hermaphroditus, who as well as being named after both parents, carried both masculine and feminine qualities.

All Hermes's children were unusual. Pan, who was half-man and half-goat, became the god of woods and shepherds. Pan's bawdy, lustful nature and his cloven hooves became associated with the Christian concept of the devil, and the words "panic" and "pandemonium" stem from his influence. Another aspect of Pan, however, was the ability to bring about states of ecstasy through playing his pipes; all who heard would be charmed. Another son, Eudorus, embodied Hermes's most positive traits—he devoted himself to caring for his flocks and those who came into contact with him. Autolycus took on his father's least appealing traits and was shunned as an untrustworthy thief and liar. Myrtilus was amoral to the extent of homicide. Each of Hermes's children reflected and magnified the many unpredictable qualities of their father.

Sibling Rivalry

As a younger brother, Hermes resented occupying what he considered a lowly position in the Olympian pecking order, and he enjoyed baiting his half-siblings. His archrival was Apollo, the golden one whom Zeus made no secret of favoring. Hermes's theft of Apollo's cattle on the day of his birth set the relationship off to a rocky start, because although he achieved his aim of keeping the prize, he was immediately brought before Zeus, who was not fooled by his protested innocence. He demanded that Hermes give his lyre to Apollo in exchange.

Relationships with his other half-siblings were, on the whole, harmonious, as Hermes was gregarious, fun-loving, and communicative. His willingness to be a messenger between the gods and on their behalf with mortals made him useful to the family, even though they were aware that his propensity for mischief did not always render him entirely trustworthy. Hermes always had an eye for chance and took the opportunity to grasp it when he could. It was his intelligence and ability to make fun of himself as well as others that made him endearing.

Archetypal Resonance

Hermes as an archetype embodies the urge to communicate and forge connections both intellectually and physically. The mind's mercurial aspect is capable of gaining insights through taking leaps across space between divergent ideas in much the same way as electrical impulses surge between neural pathways in the brain that enable connections to be made that were not previously apparent. This swift changeability can be the stuff of inspiration and innovation, but it can also lead to confused thinking. The process of accelerated learning can be used both creatively and deceptively, and it reflects the shifting facets to this archetype. Within this contrast is a necessary choice as to whether that facility is used positively or negatively—the flashes of genius that result are not bound by moral codes or a need to seek approbation from others.

As an archetype, Hermes represents the messenger, the necessity for communication that links together thoughts, ideas, and words. Sociability is an integral part of communication—in order to do it, there must be someone to communicate with or to. The Hermes archetype needs the company of others in order to shine.

Another archetypal aspect is that of rescuer. The Hermes mindset wants to help others and enjoys being useful and needed, as long as a solution can be found quickly and acted on. The urge for constant change means that the new is always welcomed—too much continuity leads to boredom, and the Hermes archetype is always in search of new experiences. Information is treasured both for its power and its use in creating increased connections. Intelligence is highly valued because stimulation is vital.

The Astronomy of Mercury

Mercury is a small planet, the closest to the sun in our solar system. It is so close that a block of lead would melt instantly in the vicinity of the side of the planet that turns its face toward the sun, where temperatures can reach 430 degrees Celsius. Yet the nighttime side of Mercury is unimaginably cold; about -180 degrees Celsius. This dual nature tells us a great deal about the extraordinary character of the planet, the archetype, and the astrological interpretation.

Also known as quicksilver, the metal mercury is unique because it does not behave as other metals do. One of its uses is in thermometers, where it allows for accurate measurement of temperature, just as Hermes is sensitive to and quick to ascertain the mental and emotional moods and temperature of those around him. However, break the thermometer and set the mercury free, and it immediately divides into numerous poisonous silver globules that run in all directions and are difficult to gather and contain.

The proximity of the planet Mercury to the sun reveals indications as to the relationship between Apollo and Hermes. The siblings blow hot and cold yet are inextricably bound together.

In Your Natal Chart

Mercury indicates how you think and communicate, processes that are reflected through whatever astrological sign the planet is situated. Your placement reveals the nature of your ability to think clearly, communicate, make decisions, come to deductions, and to form and make use of connections. The house position in your chart shows the area of your life most influenced by the information you gather and what you do with it.

Aspects between Mercury and the other planets give information as to how the intellect is used and what mode of communication comes most naturally to you. The aspects can indicate whether mental energy is swift or sluggish, free-flowing or easily blocked.

The planet's close proximity to the Sun means that Mercury's position in the natal chart is never far from that of the Sun. When it rests at its closest point to its father, Mercury's effect is intensified, bequeathing either moments of brilliance and insight that can change your mindset and those of others—conversely, it can cause mental burnout.

Self-expression is vital to Mercury. When this flows freely through other elements in the natal chart, communication is speedy and clear. If blocked, it manifests as muddled speech and thinking as well as frustration due to an inability to communicate words and ideas clearly.

Intellectual pursuits are attributed to Mercury, as are an individual's hobbies, interests, and activities along with relationships with siblings, friends, neighbors, and colleagues, reflecting Hermes's sociability. The house in which Mercury is situated also indicates short journeys and attitudes toward education.

The trickster element of Hermes is reflected in the planetary position, giving pointers as to whether it is used mischievously, as in a fun-loving character; manipulatively, as in a likeable rogue; or maliciously, as a con artist. Mercury, like Hermes, needs outlets to channel its constructive self-expression.

Rulership of Mercury

Mercury rules the astrological signs Gemini and Virgo. Its expression is different within each sign, reflecting the changeable aspects of both the planet and the archetype. Gemini is symbolized by the twins, with their attributes of dual nature, quick-wittedness, hasty speech, propensity to seek and welcome change, and shifting moods. Communication is all-important for Gemini, and their sense of fun and constant flow of bright ideas make them very popular. The Gemini mind is versatile and nonconformist. Stimulation is necessary, because Geminis become bored easily; when this happens, they may create mischief in order to shift the status quo. A keen open mind and adaptability makes them fascinating companions, though sometimes elusive and unpredictable. Hermes's charm is very apparent in this sign, and Geminis make friends easily though can tend to move on when someone new or more stimulating appears.

Mercury's rulership of Virgo reflects other aspects of the planetary archetype. Gemini absorbs information like a sponge, skimming the surface intellectually in order to pursue many diverse topics, using this information for creating connections with others in a social sense. Virgo's thirst for knowledge is more selective and directed more inwardly. The Virgoan nature investigates more deeply and is keen to constantly delve beneath the surface. Just as Hermes took on the role of messenger and helpmate to both gods and mortals, Mercury, through its Virgoan aspect, is keen to be of assistance to others. To this end, Virgo focuses intelligence on practical matters with the aim of bringing ideas to useful fruition. Communication tends to be geared toward work-related ideas and subjects, as well as service to others. Virgo is a willing listener.

Although a symbol of commerce, Hermes's caduceus is often mistaken for a symbol of healing. Hermes's caduceus is often linked to his rulership of Virgo, who tends to be health-oriented, views the body as the temple of the soul, and is diligent about hygiene and nutrition. The true symbol for healing is the rod of Asclepius, a single snake climbing a wooden staff—no wings.

In relationships, the Hermes connection is apparent in Gemini through a natural flirtatiousness and a sense of pleasure in new encounters tempered by a reluctance to be pinned down prematurely. The Virgo aspect of Hermes is more reticent and less swayed by adventure, with communication and conversation as key to gaining interest. With its ongoing friendship even after the affair was over, the relationship between Hermes and Aphrodite is typical of both Gemini and Virgo, as is the birth of Hermaphroditus—the offspring that results from the meeting of both mind and body.

Mercury's quicksilver nature determines its fluency. The expression of understanding, adaptation, and innovation act as a key to the subtle messages of other archetypes in the psyche and the natal chart, indicators of which speak most strongly through your personality.

Chapter Five

Venus—Aphrodite

Aphrodite/Venus rules Venus, Taurus, Libra, and the second and seventh houses.

The title and role of goddess of love credits Aphrodite with less than her due respect. She is the spark that ignites the inner flame of those whom she touches and transforms the internal and external perspective. Love can be vivifying or destructive. It can infuse the entire world with beauty just as it can open portals to grief and despair. Aphrodite's true gift is the transformation that occurs when she steps to the fore in the psyche.

Aphrodite reminds us that we are not solitary islands drifting in an uncaring world. Her power is a connecting emotional force that draws us toward one another and enables us to temporarily see with a deity's eyes. Through her, we shift and change and become more than we were.

The Birth of Aphrodite

There are two versions of Aphrodite's birth. In one, she was the daughter of Zeus and a sea nymph, Dione. In the other, more celebrated story, she emerged from the foam created by the genitals of Ouranos when Kronos severed them and cast them into the sea. Botticelli depicts this in his painting, *The Birth of Venus*, as she rises above the waves on a giant sea shell and is escorted to Mount Olympus by Eros, god of love, and Himeros, god of desire.

The second version of Aphrodite's birth adds to her numinous mystique as goddess of love and beauty and carries deep symbolic resonance. The combination of sexual desire that drove Ouranos to his painful fate when he approached Gaia, the sea's life-supporting properties, and the presence of the archetypes of love and desire at her birth created a being whose passions were capable of setting alight the inner spark in everything she touched. By her very nature, she was destined to embody love, creation, and inspiration.

Personality Traits

When honored, Aphrodite was the epitome of benevolence. She favored both gods and mortals and had no compunction about using her power to enchant—and in some cases, to punish. Her positive attributes embody the intense, all-encompassing joy of union, of loving and being loved, engendering a feeling of passion in the creative process and a profligacy in procreation. Her beauty inspired others to access the loftiest heights of the imagination and create works of art in all its forms that would endure, whether as visual arts, drama, dance, music, or the written word. She was helpful to those who petitioned her and could transform lives in an instant. One of her devotees was Melanion, a mortal who fell in love with Atalanta, a woman to be reckoned with.

Atalanta was beautiful and desired by many, but she was fiercely independent and reluctant to marry any of her suitors. Eventually she declared that any man who could beat her in a race could have her hand in marriage. As she was the fastest runner among mortals and the penalty for losing the race was death, Melanion appealed to Aphrodite to intercede. The goddess advised him to challenge Atalanta to a race. While they ran, with Atalanta far ahead, Aphrodite threw three golden apples in Atalanta's path. Their beauty was such that Atalanta paused to pick them up, allowing Melanion to win the race and his bride.

When not honored, Aphrodite was malicious. She was proud of her beauty and sensitive to slights. Often her revenge was directed at her antagonist through an innocent person. Aphrodite helped the hero Theseus, but he later paid dearly for betraying her.

Minos, king of Crete, asked Poseidon to send a sign to confirm his right to the throne. Poseidon sent a beautiful white bull for Minos to sacrifice to him, but Minos was so impressed by the magnificent creature that he sacrificed a lesser bull instead. Deeply offended, Poseidon cursed Pasiphaë, wife of Minos and queen of Crete, to fall in love with the bull. She mated with it and birthed a monstrous half-man, half-bull creature called the Minotaur. Minos had a labyrinth built to contain it and sacrificed young men and women to him each year. Chained to a rock as the next sacrifice to appease Poseidon, the king's daughter, Ariadne, made a plea to Aphrodite to help and was told that Theseus would marry her after killing the Minotaur. Before setting foot in the maze, Ariadne gave Theseus a ball of golden thread that would help him find his way back from the center of the labyrinth along with a sword for slaying the Minotaur.

His task accomplished, Theseus sailed away from Crete with Ariadne but refused to marry her. Instead, he abandoned her on the deserted island of Dia (now Naxos), where she was later rescued by Dionysus. Theseus married Hippolyta, queen of the Amazons, but she died after giving birth to their son, Hippolytus.

Although outraged at the slight, Aphrodite bade her time. When Theseus later married Phaedra, Aphrodite caused the unfortunate woman to fall in love with Hippolytus, her stepson. Phaedra declared her feelings to him but was spurned, so she left a note for Theseus claiming that Hippolytus had attempted to rape her and hanged herself. In his own fury, Theseus called on Poseidon to destroy Hippolytus, and Poseidon sent a wave to drag him into the depths. It wasn't until afterward that Theseus discovered the truth and was filled with remorse.

As patroness of love, Aphrodite lights an inner flame and fans it through the meeting of two people whose destinies are interwoven for good or ill. The love she inspires can elevate or destroy, and the influence of Aphrodite can create a sense of belonging or terrible unconsummated yearning.

The Transformer

Aphrodite could serve as the catalyst for self-knowledge and self-empowerment. In the story of Psyche and Eros, Aphrodite's retribution and attempted revenge brought unexpected results.

Psyche was a beautiful mortal who inadvertently offended Aphrodite because men favorably compared her beauty with that of the goddess. Aphrodite sent Eros to make Psyche fall in love with a creature of great ugliness. However, Eros fell in love with Psyche and took her away with him, commanding her not to attempt to look upon his face. Understandably curious, Psyche lit a candle while Eros was sleeping, but a drop of tallow fell on the god that startled him awake and made him fly away. In despair, Psyche appealed to Aphrodite, who gave her four impossible tasks to accomplish so that she could be reunited with Eros.

The first task was to sort a mountain of mixed seeds into separate heaps. The second was to gather fleece from the terrifying golden rams of the sun. The third was to fill a flask with water from the river Styx in the underworld, and the fourth was to take a casket to Persephone in the underworld and bring it back filled with beauty ointment. Psyche was filled with despair, but help was at hand. A colony of ants sorted the seeds. A magical reed told Psyche to gather the golden rams' wool that had caught in thorny bushes. Zeus came to her aid and sent a golden eagle to bring her water from the river Styx. The boatman at the river Styx helped Psyche to cross, and Persephone granted her request. However, the contents of the box contained everlasting slumber, and Psyche, unable to resist peeking, fell into a deep sleep. Eros came to wake her but was fearful of Aphrodite's intense grudge against Psyche. He begged Zeus for help. Zeus made Psyche immortal as goddess of the soul, and the lovers were married.

Relationships

Aphrodite had numerous lovers among both gods and mortals. She was married to Hephaestus, the club-footed son of Zeus and Hera, whose imperfection so offended Hera that she threw him down to Earth from the heights of Olympus. Hephaestus lived among mortals and built a deserved reputation as a master craftsman and smith, creating artifacts of such irresistible beauty that his services were in great demand. However, Aphrodite was constantly unfaithful to him—counting Hermes, Ares, and Dionysus among her immortal lovers. Of the mortals, Adonis was her favorite, though Persephone also loved him. When Adonis died, Zeus decreed that he should spend one-third of his time alone, one-third with Persephone, and one-third with Aphrodite.

The goddess bore children by several of her lovers. Among them were Hermaphroditus, her child by Hermes, the fierce twins Deimos and Phobos (Fear and Panic), and a daughter, Harmonia, by

Ares. In Roman myths, Cupid (Eros) is her son, though the Greeks viewed him as a primal god who came into being at the beginning of time who escorted the newly born Aphrodite to Olympus.

Aphrodite was governed by her passion, something that humiliated and infuriated Hephaestus. Although they outwardly appeared mismatched, both had extraordinary creative powers; despite her unfaithfulness, they remained together. Aphrodite's flaunting of her liaison with Ares so enraged Hephaestus that he decided to embarrass the lovers publicly. He created a net of such fine mesh that none could see it, trapped his wife and her lover in it in mid-coitus, then called all the gods to witness what he hoped would be their shame. However, the plan backfired: The gods found the situation hilarious and laughed so much that Hephaestus was forced to free the pair. Aphrodite's charms truly were irresistible.

Sibling Rivalry

Aphrodite's willingness to help made her beloved by gods, goddesses, and mortals. Her sparkling enthusiasm for life and love and her extraordinary beauty made it hard (as well as unwise) for others to deliberately cross her.

Among the family of Olympians, Aphrodite's main opponent was Hera. Aphrodite's casual attitude toward relationships and marriage antagonized Hera, whose domain was the sanctity of marriage, despite her own husband's infidelities. Hera's strong moral code was anathema to Aphrodite's urge to live in the moment and take skillful advantage of opportunities. Aphrodite ignored Hera and viewed her as a victim of her own strong morals, putting the other goddess's attitude down to jealousy.

Archetypal Resonance

Aphrodite as an archetype embodies the urge toward union, manifesting as the desire to give and receive love and to experience a sense of merging with the beloved. When we are in love, everything and everyone appears beautiful. The world is suffused with a rosy glow, and others sense the radiance around us even if they do not see it, drawn toward it like moths to a flame. The world loves lovers. Beauty is perceived even in the mundane, because Aphrodite sees through our eyes and experiences through our heightened senses. In the first flush of love, we become god and goddess in the eyes of the loved one.

When not expressed through a physical relationship, the desire to experience unity is found in artistic, creative people when an idea strikes that fires a passionate response. A painting, a series of dance steps, a poem, a manuscript, music, a song—all arise through a connection with Aphrodite when the creative act becomes an extension of the creator. Even when it is complex, the work that eventually manifests the idea is viewed as joyful rather than arduous. In periods of intense creativity, time loses all meaning except for the act of grasping what is available for the task at hand.

One aspect of Aphrodite's archetype is the yearning for harmony and warmth so fundamental to our well-being. Focus is another—the intense focus that tunes out all distractions in a conversation or undertaking an act that brings pleasure. The Aphrodite archetype shuns boredom and wishes only to experience pleasure. Monotony drives her deep within the psyche, allowing other archetypes to raise their voices until something beautiful captures her attention, whereupon she rises to the surface once more and brings a glow to the world.

The Astronomy of Venus

Venus is the second planet from the sun; a hot, radiant globe surrounded by impenetrable clouds of sulfuric acid, with a thick, dense atmosphere composed of mostly carbon dioxide. The planet Venus's greenhouse effect is akin to the heat generated by passion that makes the object of desire unknowable even as we strain to understand them. Surface volcanoes that erupt and expel sulfur dioxide cause Venus's atmospheric heat, effectively blocking the sun's light and making the planet appear luminous from the outside despite the darkness beneath its cloud cover. Undiluted sulfuric acid rains on the surface, the atmospheric pressure is intense, and it has the hottest surface temperature of all the planets—temperatures hover at around 465 degrees Celsius—because its atmosphere traps heat. Symbolically, the fires of love, when entered, are all-consuming.

As the brightest of the planets, Venus is easily seen with the naked eye and has been known in history as both the morning star and evening star. The planet's beauty and luminosity draw the eye, and lovers wish upon it for blessings and good fortune.

In Your Natal Chart

Venus in your natal chart reveals your emotional temperature in relationships with others. Your sense of beauty and harmony stems from Venus, as do artistic and romantic self-expression. The astrological sign that Venus is situated in acts as a mirror reflecting how you experience and express your feelings, revealing your approach toward possessions, comfort, and the arts. The house in which Venus sits shows your modes of expression through that particular area of life. Whether Venus brings intense passions as it does in Scorpio or as an altruistic love of humanity as it does in Pisces, this planet's reverberations are felt strongly.

Aspects between Venus and other planets show whether emotions are allowed free rein or stifled by other planets, other voices in the psyche. Positive aspects reflect the enchanting side of Aphrodite, through an openness to create love, beauty, and harmony all around. Challenging aspects can stultify the emotions and create coldness or manipulation, just as they can over-exaggerate reactions and reveal hypersensitivity, laziness, or obsession.

Feeling is imperative to Venus and to Aphrodite. When there is freedom to feel and express the emotions, the goddess brings her attributes of charm and liveliness to the fore. Blocked emotions or feelings of being neglected or undervalued cause the goddess to go to ground in the subconscious mind, where the result can be resentment, loss of self-worth, and depression.

Rulership of Venus

Venus rules the astrological signs of Taurus and Libra. Both express a desire for beauty and harmony around them, and both have an intensely sensual, loving nature. Aphrodite's expression through the earthy, physical aspect of Taurus reveals itself in an appreciation of all things that appeal to the senses. Soft fabrics and skin, delightful scents, appetizing food and drink, and melodious voices all call to Taurean sensitivities. Appearances, values, and possessions—especially those with attractive shapes and forms—are important to Taureans, who are miserable when surrounded by what they perceive as ugliness. The Taurean nature is drawn to items that are pleasing to touch and look at, and they have a keen eye for beauty.

Aphrodite's emotional nature lies beneath the surface in Taureans, and their reluctance to appear vulnerable can hold them back from expressing their feelings too openly until they are sure that these will be reciprocated. When they feel secure, they can be a rock for others to lean on, but they can also be possessive, wanting to keep what they love—people and possessions—close to them. Like Aphrodite, Taureans are loyal to those who cleave to them and are generous, giving a great deal of themselves in friendships and relationships.

The strong Taurean willpower makes them able to set a goal and plan far into the future, just as Aphrodite was willing to wait patiently for the most effective time to act after devising a plan or scheme. The story of Aphrodite and Theseus is a case in point, as she was willing to wait for years to seek revenge on Theseus through his family. Similarly, Taureans may not act immediately if they are offended or displeased but will bide their time until the moment comes when their actions will have the strongest impact.

Pleasure in indulging the senses is typical of Taureans. Quality is more important than quantity, and no expense is spared when Taureans seek to impress or seduce the objects of their desires.

When shining through the lens of her rulership of Libra, Aphrodite's love of harmony and luxury is pronounced. The goddess often bestows on Librans the quality of physical attractiveness, delight in pleasure, and a need to be liked and loved by others. Approval and popularity are all-important to Libras, just as they are to Aphrodite. Her willingness to help when petitioned is also pronounced in this sign, and her patronage of the arts flows through both Taurus and Libra. Often, Taureans will have beautiful voices, and Librans will have a natural affinity for artistic and creative pursuits that enable them to indulge a love of beauty while simultaneously experiencing a sense of union through the creative process.

Through the planet's exaltation in this sign, the Libran connection with Saturn fosters a strong sense of justice, represented in the scales that compose the Libran glyph. Fairness is imperative and, as with Aphrodite and Ariadne, they can be crusaders for a particular cause.

New ideas, intellectual stimulation, and a love of creating connections with other people make Libras sociable and delightful company. However, they can find it difficult to make decisions because they can see both sides of a choice or situation and tend to waver while they consider which is best. As with the scales that tip in either direction according to the weight of their contents, the Libra must strive to attain balance and equilibrium. Like Taureans, they prefer a peaceful life to emotional upheaval but, when crossed, both signs are capable of dire acts of retribution. Relationships are vital to well-being. Emotional discord can make them physically ill, whereas harmony around them and the attention of a loved one create a glow that spreads out to encompass all who come close to them.

Chapter Six

Mars — Ares

Ares/Mars rules Mars, Aries, Scorpio, and the first and eighth houses.

Ares embodies the impulses that call out to be followed, no matter what consequences arise. His energy, when channeled, gives rise to immense drive and achievement. The urge to action makes him hasty in speech and deed such that if left to its own devices with no specific goal in mind, turns on itself and those around him.

With this archetype, there are no sly twists and turns or convoluted machinations. Ares is the skater on the surface of life, unconcerned about checking first whether the ice is strong enough to hold his weight as he hurries to keep on moving. Because of this propensity to hurl headlong into adventure, he rarely stops to think. Passion is all. The feelings of the moment are the only consideration because Ares embodies the present, the eternal now, having no interest in a dreamy past or fictional future.

The Birth of Ares

As Zeus and Hera were Ares's parents, it was expected that he would be favored by them. Zeus had many children by different lovers, and his wife Hera had cast Hephaestus from Olympus because he was not the image of the "perfect" god; it would be only natural for Ares to be schooled as the next in line for the Olympian throne. However, his quixotic parents could not bring themselves to forge a bond with him, and Ares thus entered a world that seemed devoid of tenderness. His early experiences amplified this feeling: he was wrapped in chains and locked in a bronze jar for thirteen months—a lunar year—by two giants, Otus and Ephialtes, effectively left for dead. Hermes found and rescued him just as he was about to expire, and Ares found little sympathy from the rest of his family.

Ares was then sent to be tutored by Hermes's son, Priapus, a skilled dancer and so physically well-endowed that a fertility cult arose in his name. Ares was taught the art of dance before developing his skills as a warrior.

Personality Traits

Ares was impetuous, hot-tempered, and quick to notice slights. He had a thirst for battle and bloodshed and an innate need to prove himself. He was scorned by his fellow Olympians save for Aphrodite, who loved him and bore him three children. Their two sons, Deimos and Phobos, rode into battle with him and fought beside him, inspiring fear and panic wherever they went.

Sensitive to the rejection he had suffered at the hands of his own parents, Ares was a loyal and protective father with a determination to aid his offspring whenever they needed him. The gods' rules meant nothing to him if a child was in danger, and he ensured that the death in battle of his son Ascalaphus was swiftly avenged.

Ares had numerous children by many women. Among these, in his Roman incarnation as Mars, he fathered Romulus and Remus, twin boys who were suckled by a wolf and who grew to be Rome's founders.

The Romans worshiped and respected Ares as Mars, who embodied many attributes considered praiseworthy. To the Greeks, Ares was too uncontrollable, too ready to engage in violence, too unpredictable with his passions and frenzies. The Romans viewed Mars as the second-most important god after Jupiter (Zeus) and built temples in his honor. He was portrayed as tall, strong, and exuding masculinity, usually with a breastplate, shield, and helmet. In addition to being one of Rome's patron deities through his paternity to Romulus and Remus, he was also considered protector and benefactor of Rome's citizens.

His reputation as a natural dancer, fierce warrior, and passionate lover made him a favorite with women and a strong ally to men whom he favored. His support of the underdog was apparent through his intense involvement in the Trojan War, set in motion by Aphrodite. One of the sons of King Priam of Troy, Paris, was asked to settle an argument between Aphrodite, Athena, and Hera about who was the most beautiful. Each goddess promised him gifts in return for the prize of a golden apple. Aphrodite offered Helen, the fairest mortal woman in the world and wife of King Menelaus to Paris as her gift if he chose her. Paris could not resist and thus won Helen as his prize. Helen fell in love with him and gladly agreed to elope with him to Troy, but the gods became involved when Menelaus declared war. Ares, with his sons Deimos and Phobos, rushed to the aid of the Trojans, which did not endear him to the Greeks.

Warrior and Dancer

The combination of dance and war may appear incompatible, but both involve the necessity to connect with the passions, a trait

Ares possessed to the fullest. He was intensely physical, governed by a constant urge to action, and the intricate steps of dance could be well-used on the battlefield. A successful warrior who aims to survive has to gauge the movements of his opponent in advance and confidently take steps that enable him to avoid injury while engaging in the thrust and parry of a dance between life and death. Intuition, skill, and courage carry equal value in dance and battle; a fearless attitude is essential. Ares was no strategist; he lacked cool logic and the ability to distance himself emotionally and was therefore more strongly influenced by immediacy than long-range plans. But his loyalty to those with whom he felt a bond was absolute.

Ares's protectiveness made him a fearsome enemy. When his daughter Alcippe was raped by a son of Poseidon, god of the sea, Ares killed him instantly. Following his instincts often led him into trouble, but he was usually on the side of those who were oppressed.

Relationships

Unusual among the gods, Ares, had long-lived affairs that often produced several children with one woman despite taking many lovers. He had a reputation as a great lover because of his passionate nature, his impetuosity, his spontaneity and, like Aphrodite, his ability to focus fully on the person in his arms in the moment.

His most celebrated love affair was with Aphrodite, who bore him three children. In Roman myths, their fourth child was Cupid. They were each loyal to the other in their own way, and Aphrodite more than once interceded on Ares's behalf to the extent of physically dragging him out of harm's way. And just like Aphrodite, Ares could be jealous. When she was enamored of the handsome mortal Adonis, Ares turned himself into a fierce wild boar and killed the youth with his tusks. Even so, Aphrodite returned to Ares again and again.

Ares's children carried the qualities of both parents, especially those with Aphrodite. Their sons Deimos and Phobos inherited Ares's wildest aspects and rejoiced in the blood and mayhem of the battlefield. Their daughter, Harmonia, carried the highest qualities of both parents as the goddess of harmony. She married Cadmus, the son of the king of Phoenicia, who had offended Ares by slaying a sacred snake; as punishment, he was made to serve Ares until he was forgiven. Eventually he was freed and founded the city of Thebes and brought the Phoenician alphabet to Greece.

Sibling Rivalry

Ares was the least popular of the Greek gods. His impatient, impetuous nature and bloodthirsty aspect antagonized most of the other deities, who valued logic and order and despised emotional upheaval and outpourings. His relationship with both parents was difficult, and they neglected to stand up for him when other Olympians hurt or shunned him.

Chief among his adversaries was Athena, who took advantage of every opportunity to humiliate Ares to the point of physically attacking him. Unlike his siblings, Ares acted in the moment and spent his temper quickly, not one to bear grudges. When provoked, his fire burned fast and hot until it ran out of fuel, and then he would calm down and carry on as though nothing had happened.

Ares's involvement in the Trojan War brought him more disfavor with several of his siblings. The gods concerned themselves with mortals only when it suited them, and although the Olympian family took sides in the war, on the whole they kept their distance. Ares's stubborn and spirited support of the Trojans arose through his passionate belief in their cause and his frequent support of whom he perceived as the underdog. This support sparked many more clashes with Athena, who sided of Greece.

Archetypal Resonance

Ares as an archetype embodies the urge toward action and reaction. The surge of adrenaline, the need for physicality, and the untrammeled pursuit of impulses are typical of the Ares archetype. The needs of the body call more urgently than the needs of the mind, and slights as well as desires must be acted on instantly. The emotions are charged and there is a sense of pleasure and excitement in indulging them, whether through heated argument, brawling, or sexual activity.

There is no subtlety in the Ares archetype, and therefore none of the mind games or manipulative tendencies present in other archetypes exist here. With Ares, what you see is what you get; the passions simmer on the surface, ready to burst into flame at the slightest encouragement.

The need for physical expression can be seen in those who battle against seemingly insuperable odds. Athletes and fighters such as boxers and wrestlers all embody aspects of Ares, as they test themselves to their limits and beyond.

When placed in perspective, Ares's qualities accord with the archetypal image of maleness: the hunter who brings home sustenance and ensures the survival of his family through keeping the territory safe, the ardent lover, the protective father. Modern culture tends to favor less Arian qualities in men in favor of a softer version. Yet without the intervention of the Ares archetype, those willing to fight for a place of safety for their loved ones, our culture may not have survived. The positive aspects of the Ares archetype are factors that allow men to connect with and experience their power in a manner that is constructive rather than destructive. The upsurge of the men's movement and the enduring popularity of authors such as Robert Bly, whose book *Iron John* acted as a clarion call for men to acknowledge their masculinity, signifies that the Ares archetype is alive and still fighting, desperate for healthy self-expression.

The Ares archetype in the female psyche is channeled through raw emotional expression, assertiveness, competitiveness, physicality, and a refusal to be part of "the system."

The Astronomy of Mars

As the fourth planet from the sun and our closest neighbor, Mars engenders a deep fascination. Evidence suggests that it once held abundant supplies of water and possibly life, although now only small amounts of water can be seen at its polar ice caps. This is partly due to surface temperature variations, which shift between -133 and 27 degrees Celsius. Mars's orbit is more elliptical (or more eccentric) than most, reflecting the god's unpredictable nature.

Although about half the size of Earth, Mars has a similar-sized land-surface area because of its lack of water. Its color, due to the oxidization (rusting) of iron minerals in its surface dust, has earned it the title of the "red planet." The color of Mars reflects Ares's propensity to "see red" and to charge into the fray without forethought. Its satellites, Deimos and Phobos, two small moons that may be captured asteroids, are named after Ares's sons.

Mars is the only planet in our solar system to be inhabited solely by robotic explorers such as NASA's Perseverance Rover, which are exploring the planet with the aim of future human habitation. The qualities of the planet hold resonances with the god in both his Greek and Roman incarnations. The Roman Mars was an agriculturist before becoming a warrior, and there has been a long-term fascination with the possibility of life on Mars and whether human communities could be set up there.

In Your Natal Chart

The position of Mars in your natal chart reveals your desires and your mode of action. The qualities of action, aggression, determination, ambition, sexuality, impulsiveness, and competitiveness are expressed through the lenses of the sign and house in which Mars is situated. Levels of energy, robustness, and the ability to take initiative stem from Mars's position, and aspects to other planets show how these qualities are expressed and used.

Mars's aspects reflect the use of our energy and drive. Positive aspects enhance the attributes of courage, forcefulness, protectiveness, independence, leadership, and strength. Challenging aspects bring to light tendencies toward selfishness and self-centeredness, overt aggression, violence, and abuse.

The freedom to act is vital to Mars. Too many constraints create intense frustration that leads to fury and destructiveness. Yet too few constraints from other planets in the natal chart can also have a detrimental effect, as Mars needs gentle boundaries that give a sense of safety and help to defuse the more challenging characteristics.

In a man's chart, Mars reflects how he feels about his maleness and how he expresses it. In a woman's chart, Mars often indicates through sign and house what type of man she is attracted to, how she expresses her personal energy and drive, and in which areas of life she is most likely to be assertive.

Rulership of Mars

Mars rules the sign Aries and is co-ruler of Scorpio, having been assigned rulership of Scorpio before Pluto's discovery. The ram, symbol of Aries, illustrates the sign's headstrong qualities, whereas the scorpion reveals a fierce refusal to back down when challenged.

The Arian psyche is direct and has tremendous energy, drive, and enthusiasm that make life an exciting experience. There is a love of and desire for the new and untried, because novelty accentuates the joyful challenge of pitting the wits against the unknown. As with Ares, whose rejection by his family led him to constantly attempt to prove himself, people born under the sign of Aries are eager and impatient to make their mark on the world. Aries *must* be first and yearns to be recognized and admired by others, making for a propensity to take risks in pursuit of goals.

One element lacking in this sign is staying power. Action must bear swift results, or Aries loses interest and moves on. But the energy generated when things are going well can act as fuel that inspires others and breaks new ground.

The Arian impulsiveness and tendency to argue while not wishing to listen to others' ideas, opinions, or explanations can make them frustrating opponents. Aries can be opinionated and reluctant listeners who dislike being pinned down, always in a hurry to make life happen and accomplish the task at hand. When others insist on lengthy consideration and deliberation, Aries becomes frustrated and antagonistic and may resort to the use of verbal or physical force if they feel it is the only solution.

Defeat is anathema to Ares and to Arians. Their ability to keep going against apparently insurmountable odds makes them able to achieve a great deal. They are competitive and make strong leaders because of their courage. They are at their happiest and most loyal to their supporters when in positions of power.

When expressed through its rulership of Scorpio, the Ares archetype is a figure to be reckoned with. The emotional intensity of this combination can be a powerful force for good or ill. There are tremendous inner resources and staying power lacking in the Aries counterpart that can lead to risk-taking and a willingness to engage in death-defying acts to accomplish goals. There are no half-measures, a philosophy that can bring about extraordinary achievements or appalling degradation or destruction.

Events in myths such as Ares's slaying of Aphrodite's lover, Adonis, are a dire illustration of the Scorpio connection with Ares; the passions are so intense and inflammatory that jealousy and possessiveness can be a challenging issue. Yet this combination of archetype and sign can make them, though uncompromising, loyal to the point of giving their all for those they love.

Chapter Seven

Jupiter — Zeus

Zeus/Jupiter rules Jupiter, Sagittarius, Pisces, and the ninth and twelfth houses.

The archetype of the king and leader defines the essential qualities of Zeus. As father and ruler of the Olympians, his task is to control his unruly family and ensure that the dynasty remains powerful.

Zeus embodies the urge to create harmony in an environment through facilitating both internal and external growth. His many lovers and children were an extension of his need to be assured of his clan's perpetuity and survival. His intelligence gives him the ability to see far beyond the range of other gods and mortals. His focus is outward, on the wider vision and the future.

The Birth of Zeus

Zeus was the youngest of six children born to Rhea and Kronos, her brother and consort. Kronos had come to power through overthrowing his father, Ouranos, but when Rhea became pregnant, he heeded a prophesy that dictated his loss of power at the hands of a son. Determined not to allow this, he swallowed each of his first five children at birth.

Rhea begged her parents to help her during her pregnancy with Zeus, and on their advice she tricked Kronos, replacing the newly-born Zeus with a stone wrapped in swaddling clothes. Her youngest child grew up in safety as she sought help from Metis, goddess of wisdom, who allied him with the titans in order to defeat his father. Metis gave Zeus a potion made from powerful emetic herbs that he forced down his father's gullet, so that Kronos would vomit up the children he had swallowed. The five older siblings were Hades, Poseidon, Hestia, Demeter, and Hera, and the three brothers divided the realms between them through drawing lots. Hades won the underworld as his realm, Poseidon took the sea, and Zeus became ruler of the heavens and Mount Olympus.

Personality Traits

Zeus, in effect, became lord of the Earth as well the heavens. To the best of his ability, he was a just and fair ruler. Favoring logic and reason, he set laws that both gods and mortals were well advised to follow, and so began the age of the Olympian gods. As deity of thunder and lightning, his retribution was fierce and swift if he was displeased, but as god of rain, he vivified the earth and all living things.

As a ruler, Zeus embodied power and enjoyed exerting his authority. He attained his position through a combination of force and his ability to inspire others and earn their goodwill and cooperation. His symbolic animal, the eagle, represented his ability to take a lofty bird's-eye view, to look down from above and see the totality rather than just the details.

A natural leader and mediator, Zeus was frequently called upon to intercede in family members' affairs. When Apollo complained to him that the newly born Hermes had stolen his cattle, Zeus insisted that Hermes hand over his lyre in exchange. He cared deeply for most of his children and birthed two of them from his own body. He carried his son Dionysus stitched into his thigh until he was ready to be born, after Semele, Dionysus' mortal mother, died during the pregnancy. He birthed Athena from his forehead and furnished Artemis with her bow and arrow and her band of nymphs. He could be generous and kind, yet there was also a cruel aspect to his nature.

There are two versions of the story of the birth of Hephaestus. In one, recounted in chapter 5, Hephaestus was cast from Olympus by his mother, Hera, because he was born deformed. Another tale describes how Zeus, angry that Hephaestus took Hera's side during an argument, threw his son to Earth, leaving him permanently disabled. Zeus despised his son Ares and consistently denied him any affection.

Zeus was an expert at gathering support around him. When he overthrew Kronos, he had the help of the titans, whom he rewarded by re-establishing the freedom that Kronos had taken from them. His keen sense of justice enabled him to find ways to mediate arguments and disputes between the immortals, and he kept the peace as effectively as was possible in what would in modern terms be viewed as a rowdy and dysfunctional family. In doing so, he earned their respect.

The urge to procreate was strong in Zeus and is a characteristic of his archetypal nature as king of the gods. Producing progeny is necessary for a ruler whose goal is to establish a new dynasty, and Zeus had many children, most of them illegitimate.

Sky God

As god of the sky, Zeus could watch over Earth and observe the ways of mortals as well as gods. He invested earthly kings with their power and created and enforced laws others had to follow. His justice and retribution were swift, indisputable, and final; all who crossed him were punished, but his generous and mostly benevolent nature preferred harmony to tyranny.

The realm of sky and air denotes intellectual qualities, and Zeus favored logic and reason above all else. His dislike of Ares stemmed from his son's impetuousness and what Zeus considered a lack of forethought and common sense. Zeus's domain was the two realms of the mind, logic and abstract, thus overruling a more feeling nature. Excessive displays of emotion made him impatient and angry, but he could be appealed to through reason.

Zeus's nature was expansive, a quality reflected in his family through his numerous offspring; in his lordship over the boundless heavens; and within his mind, through the vast spaces that he occupied and ruled with a philosophical attitude.

Relationships

Before and after his marriage to Hera, Zeus had numerous liaisons with nymphs, titans, and mortal women. Many of them bore him children. Before Hera, Zeus was romantically linked with Metis, Themis, Eurynome, Demeter, Mnemosyne, and Leto—the kin of his parents. He attempted to seduce Hera through playing on her sympathies as a small, helpless bird, but she refused to become his lover and persuaded him to marry her.

Zeus's affairs were as legendary as Hera's fury and jealousy such that she was impelled to punish his lovers and their children rather than her errant husband. Although many stories are told of

Hera as the wronged and angry wife, their union was happy most of the time and Zeus always returned to her after he had strayed.

Many of the gods were children of Zeus. Among them were Hermes, through Zeus's affair with Maia; Dionysus, god of wine and ecstasy; Ares, Hephaestus, Artemis and Apollo, and the nine muses through Mnemosyne. Apart from Ares and Hephaestus, he maintained a positive relationship with his children.

Zeus also had at least one male lover. He abducted Ganymede, a handsome young mortal from Troy, and made him his cup-bearer. Zeus immortalized the youth as the constellation of Aquarius, the Water-bearer, and one of the moons of the planet Jupiter is named after him.

Sibling Rivalry

Relationships between Zeus and his siblings were generally positive, but Zeus offended Demeter, goddess of the earth and motherhood, when their daughter Persephone was abducted by Hades and Zeus ignored Persephone's cries for help. His excuse was that he had no wish to interfere with his brother's affairs, even at the risk of losing his daughter. Eventually he capitulated and decreed that Persephone would spend six months of the year with her mother and six months with Hades.

Zeus and Hera held equal power as brother and sister as well as consorts. Despite Zeus's philandering and Hera's outrage, they remained married and true to their chosen roles.

Archetypal Resonance

Zeus as an archetype embodies the role of king of the psyche; the wise, all-seeing leader who can gain the trust of others and inspire them to carry out his bidding. He was master of all he surveyed, capable, authoritarian, certain of his power and able to keep it because those around him respected him.

As creator and upholder of laws, Zeus dispensed judgements and justice and was a fair mediator in his capacity as sky god to see a situation in its entirety and come to a workable solution. His word was law, and woe betide any who ignored Zeus, as he would strike them down instantly.

The Zeus archetype manifests as a driving will aimed at gathering and consolidating power. When all is going well, peace, harmony, and benevolence reign. But in conflict, the power is held on to or retrieved at any cost, and the adversary is made to pay dearly.

A love of women is also prominent in the Zeus archetype, rather as in the case of a male animal surrounded by a selection of females that can blend new mixtures in the gene pool and assure the continuity of the species. In Greek myths, women have their place as lovers and consorts but less frequently as friends, as the Zeus archetype is a ladies' man for the pleasure he gains through the sexual act and the result of future progeny. In some of his affairs, Zeus assumed other forms. He came to Danae, mother of the hero Perseus, in the form of golden rain. Europa was seduced by him in the guise of a white bull, and Leda as a swan. This implies that the joy of conquest and impregnation were paramount to Zeus.

The Zeus archetype is not domesticated and certainly refuses to damage his mantle by taking on what he would consider "women's work." His role is that of head of his own family and the wider family of the realm he governs.

The Astronomy of Jupiter

Twice as large as all the planets in the solar system put together, this immense gas giant lies beyond the asteroid belt and is aptly named after the Roman incarnation of the sky god. Formed from gases and dust left over from the sun's formation, Jupiter is the oldest planet in our solar system, and its giant red spot is actually a storm that is bigger than our planet Earth. Jupiter has many small moons, ninety-five of which are officially recognized by the International Astronomical Union, and four large moons—Io, Ganymede, Europa, and Callisto—named after Zeus's more famous lovers. Of these, despite Jupiter's hostile, tempestuous nature and unlikelihood of the presence of life, Europa is considered to be the one place in our solar system where extraterrestrial life may be present or possible, as a liquid water ocean lies beneath its frozen crust.

The bands of color visible around Jupiter are caused by clouds of phosphorus-containing gases and jets of sulfur that swirl due to Jupiter's very fast rotation; this huge planet spins once every ten hours. Circumnavigating the planet are rings of small, dark particles that may be dust from meteoric impacts that are visible due to light from the Sun. Storms rage on Jupiter, bringing turbulent clouds of gas that fill the atmosphere with ammonia. The nature of the Jovian atmosphere reflects Zeus's rulership as god of thunder and lightning.

There is no true surface on Jupiter; the planet consists of gases and liquids. It radiates about four times as much heat as it receives from the sun, and its composition, like the sun, is mainly hydrogen and helium. Data sent by NASA's Juno spacecraft indicates that Jupiter's core is much bigger than anticipated and blends indistinctly with the metallic hydrogen that surrounds it.

Recent scientific discoveries have linked the orbit of Jupiter to sunspot cycles. Sunspots peak just after Jupiter passes perihelion, the phase when Jupiter is moving at its fastest, changing direction, and the planet's gravitational force is at its most powerful. This connection between Zeus and Apollo, the sun god and favorite son, affects us on earth— among other things, sunspots are linked to weather systems on our planet.

Around fifty light years from our solar system, a star named Beta Pictoris displays evidence of its own planetary system. Orbiting it is a planet that was discovered in 2009 and is estimated to be similar in size and characteristics to Jupiter, a finding that resonates with Zeus's control over other domains far from Olympus.

The qualities of Zeus as the most prominent god whose generative abilities were second to none are easily understood in the context of the planet that bears his Roman name. The nature of Jupiter, with its physical attributes as lord of the planets, corresponds closely with the position of the god in the Greek pantheon.

In Your Natal Chart

Jupiter's position in your natal chart reveals information about your ethics and your philosophical and spiritual (especially religious) codes and beliefs. The sign and house that Jupiter is situated in inform the person's benevolence, growth, expansion, generosity, intelligence, and goodwill. Material benefits, the respect of others, and the ability to make the most of good luck are indicated according to whether the planet's aspects are positive or challenging.

The word "jovial" (derived from his Latin name, Jove) strongly resonates with this planet; generally speaking, Jupiter's characteristic is bonhomie. As the largest planet and the archetypal ruler of the sky, Jupiter's expansive nature embodies an urge for success and recognition along with a desire to ensure that all is well with the world.

As a deity, Zeus avoided conflict and was a skillful mediator when problems were laid at his feet. The god much preferred to watch over his domains with an all-seeing eye while he enjoyed the company of those who pleased him. He took his role seriously and allowed Hera equal status in what was an otherwise distinctly patriarchal regime. He respected Athena's warlike aspect and admired her intelligence.

Jupiter embodies power that is earned and accepted naturally as a matter of course. Cooperation is viewed as a necessary quality that makes life more comfortable for all, and the wider view is always considered. Any decisions made attempt to take all sides of a situation into account—but once made, they are final.

The house that Jupiter sits in shows the area of life in which Jovian qualities are experienced and expressed, and it reflects where positive action is most likely to be channeled.

When well-aspected, Jupiter expresses expansion, optimism, generosity, solid inner faith, and good fortune ensuring that you will be in the right place at the right time to receive the many-layered benefits of its planetary influence. Challenging aspects can reveal either an authoritarian attitude that seeks to always be right and cannot admit mistakes, or it is an over-expansiveness that can lead to financial problems or unwanted weight gain.

The planet Jupiter, like Zeus, denotes an enjoyment of the good things in life. The area of the natal chart in which this planet is found is infused with energy, enthusiasm, and a positive attitude.

Rulership of Jupiter

Jupiter rules the astrological sign Sagittarius, the centaur with his bow and arrow who can move fast and aim true. The Jovian psyche is honest and open, direct in speech, and truthful to the point of giving offence, as there is less subtlety and more of a need to give voice to thoughts. A love of freedom, a tremendous pleasure in play and the company of animals as well as people, and a natural inclination toward leadership make this archetype difficult to put into a box. Whichever mindset Jupiter encompasses is likely to be continually outgrown due to its inherent need for expansion.

The capacity for deep thought and a concern for the well-being of others makes the Jovian archetype a fair and generous leader. The aspect of the conventional, a need to know that certain rules and regulations are there for the benefit of all, can manifest as rigidity or bigotry if Jupiter is badly aspected. Generally, however, there is an interest in discussion and a love for roaming the terrain of the mind, especially in the area of abstract thought; the deeper and more profound it is, the more it is welcomed and enjoyed.

A craving for adventure in pursuit of knowledge and under-standing brings a constant search for new horizons both intellec-tually and physically. Zeus's many affairs reflected his need for romantic adventures and his resistance to being kept too closely at his loyal wife's side. The Jovian psyche tends to fulfil these needs by embarking on adventures of the mind or through traveling and exploring the world.

The Zeus personality is innately positive and forward oriented. Energy is high—often exuberant—and needs to be channeled. A goal to move toward is important, particularly if attainment of that goal brings respect and acclaim from others. The need to be right can overrule the natural urge to like and be liked.

Zeus's reign over Olympus manifests as a love of a traditional, workable system. Each archetype's place was assured and tended to remain true to type. The need for a system contributed to a code for measuring and assuring good conduct and as harmonious a way of life as possible.

Jupiter co-rules Pisces together with Neptune. Jupiter's expan-sive aspects and archetype are expressed here through love, com-passion, and a benevolent attitude. A tendency to take care of others and take their needs and demands to heart can lead willingness to accept more responsibility than is healthy, as this does not create the space for allowing responsibility and autonomy in the person receiving help. Zeus was willing to intercede in disputes in order to avoid further conflict, but some of the quarrels between the deities could have been effectively resolved between themselves. As with the Jupiter-Pisces connection, Zeus takes on the role of father of all whose authority, wisdom, and beneficent nature are sometimes exploited.

Wherever Jupiter is situated in the natal chart indicates the willingness and ability to grow. The existence within the psyche of the tremendous potential for positive expression of the will encourages other internal voices to speak with more harmony.

Chapter Eight

Saturn—Kronos

Kronos/Saturn rules Saturn, Capricorn, and the tenth house.

The laws of cause and effect are attributed to Kronos. As the god of time, he reminds us that all things must pass and we must learn to take responsibility for our actions to avoid repeating past mistakes.

Kronos was the youngest son of the earth goddess, Gaia, and Ouranos, the sky god. Gaia was so fertile that Ouranos became jealous and imprisoned their children by sealing them deep within her body.

When Kronos was born, Gaia hid him from her father and waited for him to grow strong. She then armed him with a sickle of gray stone to use as a weapon. Leaping out of hiding during his parents' sexual coupling, Kronos severed his father's genitals and cast them into the sea. Aphrodite rose from the foam on the waves while the Erinyes and Furies (also known as the Eumenides) emerged from the stray droplets of blood in the air. The fierce reign of Ouranos came to an end, and Kronos released his siblings from his mother's body and took the throne.

Personality Traits

There are chilling similarities between the births of Kronos and his own son, Zeus. Both rebelled against and eventually destroyed their fathers, and they both freed their captive older siblings in order to hold on to their lives and their power as leaders. The need to survive against all odds engendered drastic measures, and Zeus subsequently allied himself with his father's siblings to forcibly end the harsh rule of his father, deploying their natural primal energy in his favor.

Once he had defeated Ouranos, however, Kronos was determined to rule alone. He chained his brothers and sisters, the titans, thereby creating the resentment that would later lead them to join forces with Zeus against him in his attempt to deny life to his own offspring.

Kronos took his authority as new ruler of the gods seriously. He married his sister, Rhea, an earth goddess cast in the mold of her mother, who, like Gaia, suffered when her husband grew resentful of her and fearful of losing his hard-won place as primary god. The first generations of Olympians were born but survived only through Rhea's determination to hide Zeus in the hope that like his father before him, he would overthrow her husband and rescue his siblings.

Kronos was stern and unbending. He intended to keep his power to himself and grasped that power jealously. Instead of sharing rulership with his siblings, he imprisoned them and thus restricted the forces of nature they embodied. He was a hard taskmaster, rigid in his approach, determined to set and maintain a status quo, allowing nothing to interfere with his autonomy.

God of Time

Kronos was the god of time who set the laws and yet was beyond them. The words "chronology," "chronic" (implying a continuing condition that persists over time), and "chronicle" (a story written in order of events) all derive. And just as Kronos/Saturn swallowed his children, so also does time swallow mortal lives and is noticed only through its passing, continuing through future generations. Kronos's rule was long, and even when his role as king of the gods came to an end, he survived and entered his next incarnation in a more beneficent form as the Roman god Saturn.

The Romans viewed Saturn very positively; it seems that in Rome he mellowed a bit and took on new qualities. To them he was Father Time, the ruler of a golden age where death and disease did not exist. In Roman tales, after his defeat at the hands of Jupiter (Zeus), Saturn made Italy his home.

Saturnalia

This festival in honor of Saturn in his role as the god of agriculture was initially held on December 17 and was later extended to the days between December 17 and December 23. In modern times, this festival is still called Yule, but its original title, Saturnalia, continues to be used in many Pagan traditions.

In contrast to the Greeks' dour image of a dark and vengeful god, Saturn had a "work hard and play hard" reputation with the Romans. Saturnalia was the most popular festival of the year, taking place when Roman farmers had finished their autumn planting.

Festivities began with a ritual during which sacrifices were made to the god and the central focus of the ceremony was a statue depicting him carrying a sickle and bonds around his feet.

Each year, the bonds were loosened in symbolic liberation, followed by feasting with an image of Saturn present at the banquet so that he could join the feast and the subsequent merriment. Gifts of wax were exchanged as symbols of the lengthening days and the return of the light. Slaves were given their freedom for the duration of the festival and were waited on by their masters. Laws were relaxed and criminals were pardoned. Dress was casual rather than formal, and public gambling was permitted. An atmosphere of jollity, equality, and relaxed social strictures reigned, often to the point of open debauchery.

Doors, windows, and even people themselves were garlanded with greenery, particularly holly, as Saturn was honored as the holly king, while Jupiter was the oak king. Gilded cakes shaped into moons, stars, and animals were made and eaten to encourage fertility in the coming year. Saturnalia was also a popular time for conception.

Relationships

The Greek portrayal of Kronos was not loveable. Slayer of his infanticidal father who then absorbed the same pattern and was in turn disempowered by his son, Kronos's ability to bond was poor. As a husband, he wanted the sole attention and devotion of his wife, which alienated her and eventually led to her betraying him in order to give life to her children … just as her own mother had with her husband. As a brother, he bound his siblings and prevented them from experiencing the freedom their father had also denied them. Ultimately, his constrictive rule cost him dearly.

His procreative powers were great and brought about a new dynasty that, try as he might, he could not prevent from coming into being. He was denied any pride or pleasure in paternity due to his ultimately well-founded fear that his progeny would take what was his. In his Roman incarnation, however, the loss of his domain led to something more beneficial to all, particularly to mortals. The golden age that Saturn heralded was a time of peace and plenty, where restrictions were lifted and the breaking of laws was forgiven rather than punished. Sharing took the place of withholding, and the god finally found a place for himself in the light—revered, respected, and loved.

Sibling Rivalry

Kronos could have invented the term "sibling rivalry." He liberated the titans from the belly of their mother only to imprison them once more to prevent them from holding any power that he considered to be rightfully his. In part, this was a punishment against them because when Gaia had pleaded for help, only Kronos was willing to come to her aid. This was not the fault of his siblings, forced as they were to endure the darkness of the Earth's depths, but Kronos had a resentful nature and no intention of dividing his realm for those beings who had inadvertently caused his mother pain.

Yet the titans' influence persisted through unions with his own progeny. Mnemosyne, goddess of memory, birthed the muses, the forces who inspire the heights of art and creativity, through her affair with Zeus, son of Kronos. Themis, titan goddess of justice and order, also entered a relationship with Zeus before he married Hera, as did Demeter, another earth goddess like her mother. Several of the sisters of Kronos had children by the son who overthrew him, and those unions populated the worlds of gods and mortals with beings who added shape and texture to the Olympian myths. Ultimately, the god of time saw his family expand to the horizons that he had attempted to deprive them of.

Archetypal Resonance

Kronos as an archetype embodies the stern father who is incapable of feeling and receiving love and affection because he never received it from his own father. More recently, we saw this in the repressed attitudes of the Victorian era, in which the father was expected to be an all-powerful authority figure whose word is law and who must be obeyed for fear of harsh retribution.

As the son who must find and display his own power in order to gain a place in the world, the Kronos archetype has the ambition, tenacity, and planning power to carry out his self-assigned tasks. But once this power is gained, a constriction occurs. What is grasped no longer brings pleasure because the fear of losing it becomes greater than the joy of ownership. In this aspect, Kronos is similar to the miser who locks away what is most beautiful and valuable to him as a way of preventing others from coveting it.

There are positive qualities, however: self-discipline, the ability to set and then reach a goal, surmounting all obstacles that stand in the way along with tremendous patience, endurance, and the knowledge that time is a commodity and can be used. The golden age of Saturn made boundaries appreciated because they created safety and stability. When restrictions were temporarily lifted and abandoned at Saturnalia, the sense of equality and freedom created a widespread state of euphoria.

In his Roman guise, we find a flip side to the Kronos/Saturn coin. As father of the gods, and as procreator and fertility symbol, Saturn represents hard work rewarded by the fruits of labor and embodies an undercurrent of sexuality and rampant life force that, though hidden for much of the time, cannot be permanently suppressed. Once the work has been done, the play can begin.

The Astronomy of Saturn

The second-largest planet in our solar system, Saturn has a similar composition to Jupiter (made mostly from hydrogen and helium) and is a gas giant like Jupiter, Ouranos, and Neptune. The planet is 95 times heavier than Earth, and its light takes just over an hour to reach us. To date, 146 moons have been registered by the Astronomical Union as orbiting Saturn.

At the center of Saturn is a core of metals such as nickel and iron surrounded by liquid hydrogen that is enveloped by liquid metallic hydrogen. The planet's density is less than that of water. The winds at Saturn's equator are the fastest in the solar system, averaging 1,200 miles (1,900 kilometers) per hour.

Saturn's rings surround the planet with a halo of what are thought to be chunks of ice and rocks coated in dust that reflect light from the sun. Both Jupiter and Saturn have a faint nimbus created by surrounding debris, but Saturn's rings are so prominent that they cannot be missed. Varying from dust-sized grains to chunks the size of an earthly house, these tiny particles of ice and rock are thought to have come from the formation of a moon that was too close to Saturn's gravitational pull to survive impact and broke into countless pieces that are now trapped in orbit around the planet. Each ring orbits Saturn at a different speed. They add to Saturn's beauty and also illustrate the symbolic resonance of the god, who in his Greek form represents restriction, boundaries, and limitation. The planet is, in a sense, a prisoner of its satellites contained within their eternal dance while he, in the center, moves alone.

In Your Natal Chart

The position of Saturn in your natal chart reveals the areas in which you become aware of responsibilities, restrictions, and limitations, and in which you possess the quality of self-discipline. Your obligations, career, and responses to discipline and hard work are all indicated by Saturn. This planet is concerned with stability, security, and a sense of order, and it gives clues as to which aspects of your life are taken seriously. It also shows your attitudes toward authority and father figures.

Status and recognition are Saturnian concerns, and a high value is placed on accomplishment. Short-term benefits are of lesser importance than achievement that endures in the longer term. Saturn is also concerned with boundaries. When positively aspected, it provides a safe container in which to work. Once those boundaries have been outgrown, new ones are set that allow for further growth and development. Saturn is a teacher who advocates self-discipline and effort toward reaching goals one step at a time. Where other planetary influences can give you the urge to run before you can walk, Saturn is cautious, sets rules and guidelines, plods steadily up the highest mountain. That determination brings you to the summit though it may take time, patience, and tenacity.

Willpower is strong wherever this planet is placed in the natal chart. It bestows an ability to concentrate; to define, set, and accomplish tasks. When aspects to Saturn are challenging, there can be tendencies to depression and low self-esteem along with the inability to accept any form of discipline or attitudes that are so repressed, tight, and restricted that they hinder growth and vitality.

Saturn completes its cycle around the sun every twenty-nine years and returns to its original position in the natal chart. Known as a Saturn return, this period occurs around the ages of twenty-nine, fifty-eight, and eighty-seven. Issues that have not been previously dealt with come to the fore during these periods. This time is sometimes naively viewed negatively and reputed to be difficult and unhappy—mainly because important life changes such as relationship break-ups or loss of a job can occur during this influence. Often there is an urge to clear the past and settle down. Some people feel an urge to start a family or a new career.

In essence, a Saturn return brings the planet's teaching qualities to the fore. If this is appreciated and worked with, it can be immensely useful. Saturn in this respect can be viewed as the rather stern taskmaster who won't hesitate to slap your wrist if you have not been paying attention to developing your potential. However, they also provide opportunities for sloppy habits to be fixed and overcome, thus facilitating growth, empowerment, and maturity.

Through its Greek aspect, the planet Saturn embodies the need to overcome small-mindedness and pettiness, to create safe boundaries, and to be aware of limitations while simultaneously understanding that too much rigidity is unhealthy and counterproductive. Through its Roman aspect, the planet acts as a reminder that necessary work leads to accomplishment and bears its own rewards. A strong Saturn can act as a framework that holds the other planetary influences in place, and that allows the maximum fulfilment of potential.

Rulership of Saturn

Saturn rules the astrological sign Capricorn, represented by the symbol of a sturdy, sure-footed goat determined to reach the top of the mountain, the pinnacle of achievement, capable of surmounting any obstacles that stand in the way. The Capricornian psyche is conscientious and determined, ambitious, and well-organized, having a powerful inner drive that keeps the person on track even when the terrain is rough.

There is a conventional slant to the Capricornian mind; a desire to follow convention, rules, and regulations, to not stand out too much in a crowd. This can initially make them appear rather solemn and constrained or even dogmatic, but if challenged they will do their utmost to come out on top. Because of their sound common sense, they think things through carefully before acting and plan their chosen route meticulously so that every contingency is allowed for to minimize any risk of mistakes or failure.

Although Capricorns may appear to be quiet, level-headed, and well-behaved, they tend to subscribe to the motto "rule from beneath," and their self-belief and tenacity makes them strive for a dominant position in both the workplace and at home. Materialistic urges stem from a craving for security, and they acquire possessions and wealth through being careful with what they have. Prudence is a key aspect of the Capricornian nature.

When young, Capricornians appear older than their years and exhibit a quiet maturity that leads them to take on responsibility easily. But as they age, they grow into themselves and after reaching adulthood, they often appear youthful in both looks and attitude.

The Kronos aspect of Saturn can manifest as stinginess and small-mindedness, and in the need to grasp out of a sense of security. The driving force of achievement is a fear of lack. The Saturn aspect manifests as a hard worker with a dry sense of humor and an underlying mischievousness that can be surprising and delightful when the outer shell of poise is penetrated.

Chapter Nine

Uranus — Ouranos

Ouranos/Uranus rules Uranus, Aquarius, and the eleventh house.

The first father of the gods and the most unpredictable, Ouranos embodies the raw power of the elements. With thunder and lightning as his tools and weapons, he impregnated Gaia—the earth, his mother, and wife—to sire the immortals only to attempt to force them back to their source. His lightning strikes manifest as both the flash of inspiration and innovation and as the touch of death that burns the target into carbon, to return to the earth who nurtured them.

The Birth of Ouranos

Gaia was the matrix from whom the gods of the future came. She herself was created through the emergence of Eros, god of love, who sprang from the void of chaos and brought a new order of life to the cosmos. The earth became the central focus for generative and procreative energy. Gaia birthed the mountains, the sea, and then Ouranos, whom she took as her consort. Heaven and earth came together and mated, resulting in the first gods, the titans, coming into being.

The fear that he would be diminished by his wife's fertility and supplanted by one of his children ultimately led to his self-destructive act of burying the offspring deep within Gaia and not allowing them to emerge. Shocked, sorrowful, and in great pain, Gaia plotted against him to take his power. She called on her children for help, but only Kronos was able to come to her aid. Ouranos was castrated and overthrown by his son. The outcome that he feared had come about.

Personality Traits

Ouranos tends to receive very negative press through some of the myths; their focus is usually on him as a jealous husband and cruel, murderous father. However, there is more to him than meets the eye.

As the first sky god, he was an elemental force whose source of grounding came through Gaia, his mother and wife. Born so closely related to the void of Chaos, he inherited much of that raw, primeval, unpredictable energy and was by his very nature uncontrollable. With Gaia, he brought worlds into being after impregnating her with thunderbolts and lightning, and the rain that issued from him fell to Earth to awaken and fertilize it. However, his jealousy of the children who resulted from their marriage and his envy of Gaia's love for them prevented them from living.

This first generation of immortals were not what Ouranos expected. The intensity of the attraction between Heaven and Earth was such that the still-chaotic energy that issued through him with all its limitless potential for forms of expression, spawning an unruly and rebellious brood that included the titans, the hecantoncheires (a trio of giants with a hundred hands each), and three cyclopes (huge creatures with a single eye in the center of their foreheads). Unable to control his offspring, Ouranos took desperate measures and sent them back to their source one by one. Kronos sprang to her aid and castrated his father, the blood from his severed genitals fertilizing the earth with his power for one final time. From this act of violence, the Furies, who unleashed violence, hatred, and anger into the world were born among others. Aphrodite, goddess of love and beauty, emerged to counterbalance the Furies' influence.

Looking beyond his negative reputation, we see the power-hungry, vicious deity become one in a difficult position. As the father of the gods, he wanted to be proud of them despite his jealousy. As father to an anarchic tribe who squabbled and warred in his presence and challenged him to the limits of his endurance, he believed he had no other choice but to dispose of them. And in doing what he felt he had to do, he justly earned the enmity and betrayal of the consort he loved.

His defeat at the hands of Kronos did not kill him; it merely rendered him incapable of procreation. He was reconciled with Gaia and remained her consort, even stepping in to give advice to his daughter, Rhea, when she begged him for help in stopping Kronos from swallowing her children at birth. The god who had been willing to deprive his children of a future was now willing to help his daughter to protect her own progeny, an indication that Ouranos did not bear grudges *and* that the myth of the envious, patricidal god was only part of his story.

Ouranos was god of the elemental forces of the storm, uncontrollable and unpredictable. No one can tell where or when lightning will hit. The earth beneath him proved to be a large target to strike, and Ouranos lacked Kronos's boundary-setting qualities that would have given him tighter control of the elements. He later bequeathed his weapons of thunderbolts and lightning to his grandson, Zeus, who used them only when necessary.

Relationships

The magnetism that repeatedly drew Ouranos to Gaia was the attraction of high abstract thought that must be brought down to earth, so to speak, to be effective. This ability to expand the thought processes to encompass vast spaces was a primary aspect of the god. By uniting with Gaia, thoughts became forms that transpired to be stronger than their parents could have possibly imagined.

Uranian energy is unconventional and feels constricted by boundaries, and Ouranos's offspring certainly exhibited what is now considered the typically Uranian dislike of authority. The need for space and change that Ouranos so forcibly attempted to meet was stunted by the new restrictions that Kronos, the embodiment of his father's opposite qualities, imposed upon him. Yet, ultimately it was this opposing force that freed him from the previously constrictive experiences of fatherhood that allowed his creative energy to be employed through mental and imaginative faculties instead.

Sibling Rivalry

Like Ouranos, his siblings—the mountains and sea—were elemental forces. These created focal points for Ouranos's self-expression. The mountains provided peaks and crannies for the god's electrical charges to travel through that resulted in changes of landscape and a playground for his power. The sea, symbol of the unconscious, provided the depth that could contain unexpressed aspects of the sky god's infinite mental energy. Gaia's children embodied the earth, water, and heavens as the conscious, unconscious, and superconscious aspects of the mind.

Archetypal Resonance

Ouranos as an archetype is the expression of the universal mind in the form of flashes of insight and intuition that can be temporarily blinding and are difficult to grasp and bring down to earth. If followed through, sudden glimpses of something intangible can lead to an intuitive understanding of universal truths. Ouranos's domain are those flashes of genius and sudden "knowing" that open the doors of perception and have led to many of humanity's most important discoveries, particularly in the sciences and spirituality fundamental to our knowledge of who we are and why we are here. These perceptions are often channeled through a glimpse of the universe as various forms of energy with patterns that are clearly—though sometimes only momentarily—seen.

The most ground-breaking scientific discoveries have arisen from lightning flashes of insight, classic expressions of the Uranian nature. The theory of gravity came about as a result of Isaac Newton pondering beneath a tree as he watched an apple fall to the ground. Albert Einstein's famous equation $E=mc^2$ resulted from a daydream he had about what it would be like to ride on a beam of light. Uranian gifts most commonly reveal themselves when the mind is in a relaxed, receptive state. There are many examples of the expression of Ouranos's archetypal resonance in the sciences, arts, and in spiritual insights, yet ideas alone are not enough. They must be grounded, brought to earth and made explainable, solid, and real in order to be useful—just as Ouranos needed Gaia to express himself fully.

This archetype has wild and unpredictable energetic qualities. It is difficult to grasp because it battles against constraints. Thought must be allowed to fly free and soar above uncharted territory, but the seeds that fall from these excursions can be caught and planted in the earth, nourished, and allowed to develop into new and wondrous forms whose shoots spread and diversify into ever-widening areas.

The Astronomy of Ouranos

A planet classified as an ice giant, Ouranos has more than twenty-four small moons. The atmosphere is composed mostly of hydrogen and helium, and large quantities of methane give the planet its distinctive blue-green color when viewed from space. Ouranos houses a small rocky core approximately the size of planet Earth. Its weather is extremely cold and windy and changes only imperceptibly over decades unlike that of Jupiter, which is subject to continuous violent storms. One year on Ouranos, one cycle around the sun, is the equivalent to eighty-four Earth years. Yet even with its tremendous distance from the sun (roughly twenty times that of Earth), Ouranos responds to our fiery luminary by experiencing seasons. In the springtime, wisps of cloud appear in the upper atmosphere, gather, and shed their contents on the planet's surface, much as Ouranos fertilized Gaia with storms and rain.

Ouranos was discovered in 1781 by William Herschel, a British astronomer, using a homemade telescope set in the garden of his home in Bath, England. The place is now a museum, and you can stand beside the telescope that revealed the discovery of a far distant planet. Initially the planet was named Herschel, but its name was changed to Ouranos as that name stuck and the god's unpredictability accorded with the strange anomalies of the planet's orbit.

The orbit of Ouranos is erratic and unusual because the axis is tilted and lies in the same plane as its orbit. Because of this, Ouranos moves around the Sun in a motion that resembles a corkscrew, whereas other planets spin on themselves rather like a child's spinning top. It is thought that Ouranos was involved in a collision early in its formation that knocked off a piece of it and created its extraordinary manner of travel through space. The myth of Ouranos's castration by Kronos and the god's subsequent withdrawal from the orbit of the titans and Olympians is reflected in the skies.

In Your Natal Chart

The position of Ouranos in your natal chart shows how you experience and express urges toward freedom of self-expression as well as your need to assert your individuality. The area of the chart in which Ouranos is situated reveals clues about your soul purpose in this lifetime, especially with respect to understanding why you are here and what you can accomplish to experience fulfilment. In the signs, Ouranos has a powerful generational influence due to the planet's slow movement, whereas its position in the houses and aspects show its influence on the individual.

This planet gives an intuitive link to the universal aspect of the mind, and the sign and house that it rests in are indicators of how that connection with the source of thought and ideas is made. The goals and aspirations that provide impetus to the defining of your sense of inner purpose (rather than Saturn-ruled physical, material aspects) derive from the influence of Ouranos.

The types of friendships that you seek and find enlivening are also attributed to this planet, because Ouranos rules group activities and situations that allow like minds to connect with each other. Through these connections, ideas are swiftly disseminated and thought processes affect entire generations and cultures rather than individuals. The internet's capacity to provide links and information to and between all, its connections offered through social media as well as instant global communication, and its speed of accessibility are all a powerful example of Uranian energy.

As the planet of magnetism and the unexpected and unconventional, Ouranos brings together the unusual and unlikely that together create new possibilities. There is an elemental aspect to this planet's influence. Flashes of attraction, insights, eccentricity, and revelations are its domain. The urge to discover, to seek out the unknown and unusual to learn and communicate that knowledge is typically Uranian. With its combination of science and insight, astrology itself is ruled by Ouranos.

Natal position and aspects can reveal gifts and interests in the sciences, particularly in areas such as electromagnetism and quantum physics. The god's generative ability that emerges through the union of opposites, of heaven and earth, can spawn monsters as easily as it can birth ideas that benefit all.

Challenging aspects can manifest as a desire to be different at any cost, outrageous behavior for the sake of it, and as stubbornness and lack of consideration for others' feelings.

There is a keen intelligence that underpins the Uranian energy that when coupled with humanitarian attitudes makes for stimulating and fascinating friends whose joy in discovery touches those around them.

Rulership of Ouranos

The astrological glyph for Ouranos looks like an aerial antenna set atop a circle, the symbol for the heavens connecting with the earth. Ouranos is ruler of Aquarius, whose pictorial symbol is of the water bearer who pours out the forces of life and spiritual energy that vivify all it touches. The Romans connected this astrological sign with Ganymede, the beautiful Trojan youth whom Zeus/Jupiter fell in love with and immortalized in the sky. In modern symbolism, this is represented as a female form, but the Romans considered Ganymede to have been the force to bring life-giving rain at the command of the thunder and lightning that Ouranos hurled through the skies.

Aquarius carries attributes of love of humanity, independence, originality, and eccentricity. As an air sign, Aquarians are thinkers. Whereas the thought processes of their fellow air signs (Gemini and Libra) are concerned with making connections with people to satisfy curiosity and find balance, Aquarians are focused on discovering and communicating higher truths that will benefit humanity across a broad scale.

The extraordinary characteristics of Ouranos are generated through a love for the new and unusual as well as the quest for a higher expression of truth. Ouranos brought into being a tribe of strange creatures who populated the earth and could not be suppressed or oppressed despite his efforts. He was the first father, the creator of forms who emerged through his connection with a greater and more complex source than his mother and consort. When there is a link with the creatrix of all possibilities as with Ouranos and chaos, the unusual is bound to emerge and must be allowed its expression with safe boundaries to prevent that energy from spiraling out of control. The Aquarian mind holds a natural connection with this source and is constantly seeking new ways to explore and express its energy.

Friendships are important to Aquarians, though they tend to avoid alliances that are clingy, needy, restrictive, or overly demanding. Independence is paramount. They prefer to steer their own course; if opposed or blocked, they rebel against those who hold them back. Their free-thinking Uranian minds can make them a mystery to other, more conventional types, and their quirks and eccentricities are viewed as interesting or odd, depending on the observer.

The relationship between Ouranos and his offspring is an apt illustration of the reluctance of Aquarians to kowtow to authority. His children rebelled against him and were unruly and difficult, refusing to be judged by his standards. Ouranos's response to his fear of their attempts to assert control over him was to detach himself utterly from them, to bury them out of sight and mind. Aquarian energy dislikes being contained or restrained and reacts strongly against any attempts by others to do this. Relationships can have an impersonal edge to them; though enjoying stimulating company, Aquarians need the freedom to roam the vast inner regions of the mind. They can then bring the gifts they find back to the earthly, worldly realm and anchor the abstract thoughts into tangible, useable forms.

Chapter Ten

Neptune — Poseidon

Poseidon/Neptune rules Neptune, Pisces, and the twelfth house.

Poseidon guards his secrets closely, hiding them in the numinous realm of the subconscious. Dreams and nightmares, visions and illusions are his domain. The mind that seeks to go beyond these, to discover the truth behind the seductive trappings of Maya, illusion, must first dive into Poseidon's realm and risk all to bring the pearls of wisdom to the surface. Too shallow a dive and only confusion waits; too deep and madness beckons. Poseidon makes his own rules and breaks them when he wishes to. Make a friend of this elusive god, however, and gateways into mystery open. The ecstasy of spiritual communion, the wordless song of the self is reached when Poseidon chooses to turn the key and allow access to the deep self.

The Birth of Poseidon

Poseidon was one of the sons of Kronos and Rhea, alongside Hades and Zeus. In the best-known version of the myths, he was swallowed by Kronos at birth and was later rescued when Zeus challenged his father and forced him to regurgitate his siblings using potent herbs. The three brothers drew lots for the realms, where Poseidon won the sea and from then onward ruled the waves. His emblems became the white horse, the bull, and the trident. White horses with golden manes drew his chariot over the sea (even now, the frothy crests of waves are called "white horses" in his honor), and he used his trident to stir the waves into a frenzy, creating storms when he was angered. The bull represents his stubborn nature.

Another version of Poseidon's birth tells that Rhea substituted a foal for the newborn child. Kronos, realizing he was being tricked, took Poseidon and threw him into the sea, expecting him to drown. Instead, he survived and the waters became his domain.

Personality Traits

Poseidon was a tempestuous god. Like the sea, he could be peaceful just as often as he could be violent and vengeful, with a tendency to quarrel with others and seek retribution if he did not get his own way. He brought forth raging storms that destroyed all in their path, deprived areas of water if he was offended (something that happened quite easily), and was a fearful opponent. When in a calmer frame of mind, he would lull the waves and dissipate storms by riding his chariot over the sea.

If he discovered he had been deceived, he grew fierce. When King Minos of Crete asked Poseidon for help, the god sent a white bull from the waves, stipulating that it was to be sacrificed to him. But the bull was so beautiful that Minos hid it away and sacrificed another in its stead. In revenge, Poseidon caused Minos's wife, Pasiphae, to fall in love with the beast and mate with it. From this union came the Minotaur, a fierce half-man, half-bull creature that demanded human flesh. King Minos built a labyrinth as a home for the bull, and each year sent young men and women as sacrifices. Eventually, with the help of Aphrodite, and Minos's daughter, Ariadne, Theseus entered the labyrinth armed with a sword and a ball of golden twine to slay the Minotaur. When Theseus abandoned Ariadne, Aphrodite took revenge on his family, creating a tragedy that Poseidon was drawn into by sending a wave to sweep Theseus's son to his death in the sea.

As well as the sea itself, Poseidon ruled shifts within the earth and could cause earthquakes. His sovereignty over underground springs enabled him to nourish the earth from beneath or, when enraged, to flood it. His earlier name as husband of the earth bears connotations of a pre-Olympian god worshiped in Pagan traditions as a consort of the Earth goddess.

Although feared by gods and men for his rages and his ability to hold grudges over lengthy periods of time, Poseidon had a gentler side to his nature. He favored Castor and Pollux, twin sons of Zeus and Leda, who were conceived after Zeus seduced Leda in the form of a swan. When Castor died, he was sent to the underworld realm of Hades; Pollux was taken to Olympus. Pollux mourned the loss of his twin so deeply that the gods took pity on them and made them both immortal. They agreed to divide their time between the underworld and Olympus, and Poseidon made them both guardians of sailors. Eventually they were set in the heavens with a constellation named after them—Gemini, the twins.

In the southern corner of ancient Greece lived the Aethiopians, people of harmony and tranquility whose feasts were legendary. Deeply touched by the feasts held in his name, Poseidon visited the Aethiopians to relax and surround himself in their gentle energy.

He was a complex god, ruled by his emotions. Like Ares, his fellow Olympians disliked him because he expressed his feelings forcefully rather than adopting a cooler, more logical stance. His domain represents a person's emotional life as well as the unconscious, reflecting Poseidon's many moods.

Ruler of the Deep

Even when the surface of the sea appears to be peaceful, the depths are unknowable. No light reaches the seabed, and there are still areas that are inaccessible and unexplored, even with modern technology. The pressure is intense, capable of crushing us out of existence, and strange creatures inhabit the darkness. Poseidon was the only god to have access to this domain, and he preferred to keep its mysteries silent and secret. The emotional resonance Poseidon holds is illustrated in the saying that "still waters run deep." Yet Poseidon could ride the waves, driving his chariot to soothe them or stir them into a frenzied, deathly dance. Like the sea, there was an unfathomable quality to him, and even now, both god and the sea keep many of their monsters and treasures hidden where none can reach them.

The subconscious mind is the resting place for the monsters that lurk within the psyche; the home of primeval fears that color our minds with hues so subtle that we only notice them when they exert control over the way we live our lives. But there are also gifts and treasures here. The creatures of the deep create their own forms of light and find their own way by it. They inhabit a world that we can only imagine, that allows us entry through the vision-making faculties of the mind, fueled by the powerful emotions that open portals into the deep self.

Relationships

Like most of the gods, Poseidon had many lovers. He fell in love with Amphitrite and, when she hid from him, pursued her to ask her to be his wife. Delphinus, the dolphin, interceded and pleaded

Poseidon's case, and Amphitrite agreed to marriage. In gratitude, Poseidon placed Delphinus among the stars as a constellation.

The marriage of Poseidon and Amphitrite was similar to that of Zeus and Hera. Poseidon's frequent straying made Amphitrite so enraged that she, like Hera, took revenge on the women her husband lusted after. A few escaped her vigilant eye. Demeter, out searching for her daughter Persephone after Hades had abducted her, was pursued by Poseidon and transformed herself into a mare so that she could hide in a herd of horses. Poseidon took on the form of a stallion and mated with her.

Poseidon and Amphitrite had a son and two daughters, and he sired numerous children by other women, some of them monsters who inherited his more vindictive qualities. Like Ares, he was devoted to his sons and always took their side.

Sibling Rivalry

Poseidon was a jealous god. He coveted the throne of Zeus and frequently attempted to overthrow his brother but was always defeated. In one tale, he enlisted the support of Hera and Athena when Zeus was out of favor with them, and they helped him bind Zeus in chains, but the leader of the gods broke free and Poseidon returned to his watery realm.

His relationship with Athena was usually stormy. Her coolness infuriated him, and his temper made her hostile. When he seduced a beautiful young woman named Medusa in one of Athena's temples, the furious goddess turned Medusa into a monstrous gorgon with snakes for hair whose gaze would turn mortals to stone. The unfortunate woman was later slain by the hero Perseus, son of Zeus and Danae, who was conceived when Zeus visited her in the form of a golden shower. Athena advised Perseus to use his shield as a mirror to avoid being turned into stone by gazing directly at

Medusa's face. When he beheaded her, the winged horse Pegasus sprang from her neck; his relationship to Poseidon with his equine connection apparent.

Poseidon competed with Athena for rulership of the city of Athens, and both bequeathed a gift in order to persuade its citizens to choose them. Athena gave an olive tree, while Poseidon donated a spring. After the citizens chose Athena, Poseidon sent a flood to surround the city in a rage.

His ability to control underground springs and earthquakes was a source of great worry to Hades, who feared that the roof of the underworld would collapse and destroy his domain.

Archetypal Resonance

Poseidon as an archetype embodies the realm of deep emotion and bears a darker aspect to the desire for the love Aphrodite symbolizes, of whom he is an archetypal harmonic. Poseidon's gift is the ability to dive beneath the surface, go beyond outward forms, and engage intuitively with unplumbed areas of the mind and feelings that are not easily accessible. The ability to dive this way is both a blessing and a curse. The emotions can be overwhelming if no constructive channel can be found for their expression. Poseidon's feelings ruled him, releasing in torrents of rage or waves of love and creativity. He demanded respect, which does not come easily in many cultures, ancient or modern, where excessive displays of emotion are frowned upon. Yet this access to the regions of the mind dark and fathomless, illuminated by creatures who have never seen the light of day, enables us to tap in to and discover the mysteries of the inner self. These regions are sensed rather than seen; they can be terrifying or profound, depending upon a person's willingness to acknowledge and permit their presence in the psyche.

This intensity can allow entry into the numinous realms of inspiration and creativity. We interpret the deepest regions of the mind through symbols, the language of the subconscious. An intuitive connection with this language gives rise to an understanding of our inner nature and the expression through poetry, music, art, and mysticism.

The Poseidon archetype's positive aspect is the gentle, dreamy mystic; a clear, uncluttered conduit that the muses can be channeled through. Intensity of feelings brings about great highs and lows, but from these come tremendous insights and a plethora of artistic expression that more earthy types find touching and resonant. As a higher energetic octave to Aphrodite, whose birth took place within his realm, this element brings a deep sense of compassion and empathy, along with connection to an inner wellspring that pours forth directly from the source of life.

The negative Poseidon archetype manifests as repressed emotion that, when the limits of containment have been breached, has no alternative but to burst forth as rages or fits of weeping. Because Poseidon is a shadow aspect of Zeus, feeling supersedes logic and there are frequent experiences of loss or defeat over issues of power, ownership, or leadership. Those who oppose Poseidon are left to deal with an implacable and vindictive enemy.

Another expression of Poseidon is the wild, instinctual masculine force that intuits situations and cannot be put in a category or tamed. The power Poseidon holds over us is fueled by strength and courage and is as tumultuous as the sea, making us fearless in the face of opponents, even in defeat.

The Astronomy of Neptune

The planet Neptune is an appropriate astronomical mirror for the Greek Poseidon and his Roman counterpart. With its atmosphere of helium and hydrogen, this gas giant appears blue (due to methane) from a distance with fluffy white clouds. But like the surface of the sea, its weather systems are all that can be seen of the planet's surface. Beneath those clouds are gases and liquids that seethe and boil. Storms and hurricanes rage across its surface carrying supersonic winds that reach up to 730 miles (1,170 kilometers) per hour. Dark spots are visible through the atmosphere, marking the presence of storms of unimaginable velocity and fury. These are thought to be hurricanes, each containing an eye in its midst that opens into areas of the atmosphere that cannot be seen from above the planet. One year on Neptune around the sun is equivalent to 165 Earth years; time moves slowly in the realms of the immortals.

Neptune has sixteen known moons. Its largest, Triton, named after a son of Neptune and Amphitrite, is the only moon in our solar system that circles its host planet in a retrograde orbit, a direction opposite to Neptune's rotation.

As with Jupiter, more heat is generated within Neptune than is received from the sun. Astronomers theorize that this arises from a process wherein Neptune contracts through the force of its own gravity to stir up the interior of the planet and create the intense movement of the clouds that sweep past high above. These characteristics reflect much of Poseidon's mythology: the unknowable qualities, the storms that rage, the hurricanes whose eyes calmly gaze into mystery. Like the god himself, the planet refuses to give away too many of its secrets. And in the calmer regions, it is the dazzling blue of the sea on a tranquil day, where clouds galloping across like white horses leave only traces of their passing.

In Your Natal Chart

The placement of Neptune in your natal chart indicates how you experience and express the deep emotions as well as how you access your mind's image-making faculties. The planet's nebulous qualities and the god bring increased intuition, depth of feeling, premonitions, and mystical insights through Poseidon's rulership of the subconscious mind. From these depths emerge symbols that can be interpreted and understood. Poseidon allows his secrets to be unveiled so long as you are willing to dive deep and react with wonder, rather than fear, to what you see.

When suppressed by challenging planetary aspects, Neptune manifests as either sudden rages and eruptions when frustrations are encountered, or as a state of introversion in which feelings are buried deep beneath the surface and are not allowed credence until they erupt, boil over, and create havoc.

When channeled constructively, Neptune brings a connection with inner space and a luminous source that enables glimpses of beauty in all forms. Surfaces are breached, and even the apparently mundane is seen to have a magical place in the world.

If not allowed expression, Neptune's longing to penetrate mysteries can become an urge toward escapism, particularly through the abuse of alcohol and drugs. The experiences these substances provide are illusory and, like the negative aspect of the god, devious. The sense of connection with the deep self is only temporary and ultimately becomes a trap that drives one further from their true nature.

When tapped into through meditation, visualization, use of imagery, or creativity, Neptune bestows the gifts of insight and compassion. Artists and filmmakers tend to have a strong Neptunian connection through their ability to envision and understand how the mind works, and they're able to create symbolic representations that others can relate to at a feeling level.

As a deity, Poseidon was shunned, misunderstood, and even feared by his family. His unpredictability, his longing for acceptance—that led him to attempt to gain power through grasping what others had, in order to be viewed as similar—proved unfulfilling and frustrating. A strong Neptune influence in the natal chart can best be expressed through an acceptance of differences and appreciation of the potential of whatever gifts are at hand. The most beautiful works of art are those that emerge through passionate emotion. The most inspirational people are those who are in tune with their positive Neptunian qualities—those who are not afraid to be different and who allow their voices to soar freely above the drone of conventionality.

Rulership of Neptune

Neptune rules the astrological sign Pisces. The symbol of two fish swimming in opposite directions reflects Neptune's dual nature—the turbulent, manipulative type who uses tears as a weapon and the compassionate mystic whose empathy breeds altruism and gentleness. Both of these elements are present in Piscean nature, although one will be more dominant than the other depending upon the position of the planet in the natal chart. Their watery nature makes Pisceans sensitive and ruled by their emotions. The symbol of the fish also illustrates an element of indecision in their makeup. Their desire to go with the flow and their innate sympathy toward others can make them indecisive about which direction is best to move in. They are patient and kind, but when provoked beyond their limits they can display astonishing outbursts of emotion.

Pisces has a tendency toward mood swings, with displays of the heights of optimism followed by the depths of pessimism. The Neptunian link with the sea emphasizes this unpredictability, flowing and ebbing like the tide, calm one moment and engulfed by stormy waves soon after. The Piscean need for retreat to a place of peace and solitude to gather their energy and equanimity reflects Poseidon's delight in the sanctuary of Aethiopia.

Pisces can appear dreamy and otherworldly, impelled by internal visions that those around them find difficult to decipher. They dislike being pinned down and resist others' categorization. Their imagination is active and fertile, and their visionary faculties are strong. These tendencies can manifest as artistic or poetic abilities, or through sculpture or dance. The Poseidon influence often gives a feeling of needing more control, of not being in charge of their own destiny just as the god attempted to go beyond his own designated boundaries and rule other realms. Pisces's boundaries are nebulous and undefined, and it can be difficult for them to know whether what they are feeling is from within them or has been absorbed from others around them.

The Piscean psyche longs to encompass the mysteries of life and to be encompassed by the feelings of homecoming generated through a connection with the source. Like Poseidon, they sometimes feel misunderstood but hold great power within them.

Chapter Eleven

Pluto — Hades

Hades/Pluto rules Pluto, Scorpio, and the eighth house.

The essential quality of Hades is access to the underworld of the self; the repository of all that has gone before, the depths of the unconscious both personal and collective. Here lay the blueprints of all previous experience with their gifts and terrors and potential for regeneration.

The dark of Hades's realm is the dark of the earth, where seeds must germinate in solitude and silence before pushing upward into the light. This dark is fearful only because it is unknown, unfamiliar. It takes what is no longer needed back into itself, pares down the bones of outward forms so that new, healthy flesh may grow on them. As lord of the dead, Hades opens the portal to the birth of the new self. He allows no looking back, no fond glances toward the past. He bequeaths the awareness that death is only another adventure that leads to rebirth.

The Birth of Hades

Hades was one of the six children of Kronos and Rhea, swallowed at birth by his father. After Zeus forced Kronos to regurgitate his siblings, Hades joined with Zeus, Poseidon, and the titans to battle with his father. The victorious brothers then drew lots to divide the universe into three: the heavens, the sea, and the underworld. Hades became ruler of the underworld, the realm of shadows where souls journeyed to after death.

Personality Traits

Hades was the quietest of the gods. He chose to stay secluded in his realm and in Greek myths was known to have left the underworld twice only: once to abduct Persephone and once to travel to Olympus to be healed of a wound inflicted on him by Heracles. He avoided the conflicts and dramas that the majority of his family reveled in, having no urge to seek adventure. He owned a cap that could make its wearer invisible and used its powers to retain his privacy, preferring his own company to that of others.

The Greeks were superstitious about using his name, lest they inadvertently invoke him. He inspired awe rather than fear and his titles included "the Unseen One" and "the Rich One." The Romans chose to call him Pluto, a derivative of *Plouton*, another Greek name. Plutonium, a chemical element appearing as a silvery radioactive metal used in atomic physics, is also named after the god, as the planet Pluto's discovery marked the beginning of the Atomic Age.

Unlike the rest of his family, Hades had few romantic liaisons. His reclusive temperament set him apart. With only a few notable exceptions, those who entered his realm went there because their mortal lives had reached the end, and it was rare for him to leave the underworld and return to the light. The god and his domain both bore the same name and were closely identified with each other.

The psychological realm of Hades is the unconscious mind and encompasses both the collective unconscious (the storehouse of all memory) and the personal unconscious (the repressed memories and thoughts only seen and felt as shadows in the conscious mind). The underworld Hades inhabited was a place where the shades of the dead went to rest. Later, Christians would link the underworld with Hell, named after the Norse goddess Hel, queen of the Nordic underworld. Yet there is no link between the realm of Hades and that of the Christian devil. Though the Greeks considered him stern and grim, he was not viewed as evil or malicious. His realm did not welcome visitors other than those who belonged there, but it was not a fearsome place, and Hades had no interest in the worlds beyond his own. Recluses throughout history have a strong Hades aspect, shunning the company of others in order to maintain their solitude.

Hades was god of wealth as well as lord of the underworld. The riches hidden deep within the Earth—fossil fuels, gemstones, precious metals—belong to him. Although he possessed untold riches, he valued them silently without feeling a need to make showy displays. The god carried his position with silent dignity, except when he fell in love with Persephone.

His rulership of the areas of dark and shadow and the depths negotiated as an initiatory experience gave him a reputation for being silent, stern, and withdrawn that in modern times could be considered to be depressive. Hades certainly lacked a sense of humor; identified as one, both god and realm were serious business.

The Realm of the Dead

Hermes would accompany the souls of the dead to the underworld when their mortal lives ended. First the River Styx had to be crossed, and the souls took with them a coin to pay the ferryman who waited there to take them on the next stage of the journey, across the dark water. At the other side were the gates to the underworld, guarded by Cerberus, a massive and terrifying three-headed hound who allowed entry but permitted none to leave. Once past the gates, the souls were judged before Minos, Rhadamanthus, and Aeacus before being permitted to fully enter Hades's realm.

The shades of the dead remained in the underworld as shadows of their mortal selves. Some stayed forever; others drank from the waters of Lethe to make them forget all that had gone before to be reborn again as mortals.

Hades was divided into three areas: the Plain of Asphodel was where most souls were taken. A few fortunate ones went to Elysium, the islands of blessed immortality. Tartarus was the equivalent of the Christian and Buddhist hell-realms, where those who had committed evil deeds were imprisoned and punished.

The entrance to Hades was said to be the mouth of a cave in an isolated area at the very edge of the world, though Hades could open the earth to appear or disappear into it whenever he chose.

Relationships

The only sexual relationship Hades had was with Persephone, daughter of his sister Demeter and brother Zeus. He abducted, raped, and married her, but Persephone's unwillingness to give herself to him and her anguish at being torn from her beloved mother meant that the forced marriage began joylessly. Later, when Hermes came to fetch Persephone, an agreement was formed between husband and wife. Persephone ate seeds from a pomegranate that Hades gave her, and kept her promise to divide her year between time in the underworld and the light.

Before he met Persephone, Hades desired Minthe, but she turned into a mint plant and was lost to him before he could touch her. Another who eluded him was Leuce, who became a white poplar tree. Hades could be content with celibacy, but he was also capable of forming deep and enduring attachments, as he did with Persephone despite his initial abominable treatment of her. His silent, brooding demeanor did not make him skilled at the hearts-and-flowers approach to romance. Hades desired little but ensured that he took what he wanted. Although his brothers Zeus and Poseidon forced their attentions on women, it is Hades who is renowned and reviled for his early treatment of Persephone. With the more extroverted gods, such behavior was viewed as an aspect of their nature; it was considered that all women were theirs by right of their sovereignty. Because Hades was the quiet god, his obsession with Persephone was more noticeable than his brothers' philandering. Unlike Zeus and Poseidon, he was faithful to his wife after marriage.

Sibling Rivalry

Hades avoided contact with others, including his siblings, as much as possible. He refused to engage in power struggles and had no interest in ownership of any domain other than his own. When Hades abducted Persephone, Zeus pretended not to hear her cries for help as she was taken to the underworld. If his loyalties were to be divided, he was on the side of his brother, and he later ignored the pleas of Persephone's mother, Demeter, to intercede and insist on Persephone's freedom.

Poseidon's rages and storms made Hades nervous. He feared that his brother's tempestuous nature would bring down the roof of the underworld and render him without a home and domain. He took his responsibilities as king of the shades seriously and was aware that if disaster struck, there would be no place for the souls of the dead to inhabit.

The other deities viewed Hades as one who was set apart from them, and his lack of interest in them and solemn nature ensured that he was not included in their activities. Hades was a loner who relished the freedom from strife that his aloofness brought him.

Archetypal Resonance

As god of the underworld, Hades embodies the psyche's shadowy aspects; the deep, dark, hidden areas of the unconscious mind. Even when he ventured above the surface, he wore his cap of invisibility, an indication that even when acting at a conscious level, his motives remained hidden from those around him. Whereas Poseidon/Neptune is the deep self's subconscious aspect that makes itself known through turbulent emotions and intuitive insights, the realm that Hades inhabits is buried beyond the reach of the everyday mind.

This archetype is the strong, silent, brooding element within that needs peace, quiet, and solitude in order to be at home. The darkest area of the psyche holds the key to buried fears and that which is too shameful or distasteful to be expressed. These qualities exert an invisible control over external emotions and reactions from their resting place deep within. Memories are suppressed but not obliterated, reflected as fragments of associations that outwardly appear insignificant but unconsciously hold great power.

The Pluto aspect of Hades as god of wealth can manifest as those who have gained riches but reject the outer world's social niceties. At a more fundamental level, the riches Hades symbolizes are the jewels of the soul. In truth, a diamond is a chunk of carbon that has been compressed by enormous pressure within the depths of the earth. It is hard enough to resist attempts to smash it, and when removed from its womb and cut and polished, it becomes a highly prized gem of great beauty and value. The Plutonian aspect of Hades is similar to the diamond and is accessed through the search for the essential self—the jewel within. The quest to find this jewel must be undertaken through entering the darkness and silence of Hades, for only through knowing and understanding the shadow can the esoteric realms of the self be fully revealed and integrated.

Experiences of loss and depression drive us downward into areas we find frightening because the self of self becomes temporarily lost. Yet the hero element within us must make that descent into the underworld to discover hitherto undreamed-of strengths and bring them back into the light of everyday life. This is a daunting prospect due to the fear that once down there in the shadowy dark, we will become trapped and unable to return; we will drink the waters of Lethe and forget who we truly are. When we experience despair, we see a glimpse of Hades's realm in its interpretation as Hell. Within the domain of this god we are subjected to the thrall of buried fears and desires, impulses and memories we would prefer to forget. But through this route we can also connect with the root patterns of the archetypal energies expressed in our personalities and can experience a journey of astonishing self-discovery and beauty.

The Astronomy of Pluto

Astronomically, Pluto has been on quite a journey of identification. Discovered in 1930 after predictions of its presence as early as 1905, and marking the beginning of the Atomic Age, Pluto was initially named as a planet. Years later it was re-categorized as an asteroid, and in 2006 it was reclassified as a dwarf planet, its current identification.

Pluto is the smallest planet in our solar system at only two-thirds the width of our moon with an unusual composition. NASA's

New Horizon space probe made a close flyby of Pluto in 2015. Scientists believe that Pluto has a rocky core deep below the surface of an ocean of water encapsulated by a layer of ice. The surface crust is composed of several ices, mostly nitrogen, with mountains of water ice reaching up to 11,000 feet (3,500 meters) high, and elements of methane and carbon monoxide ice. This immediate impression bears similarities to Hades' cold, hard, detached reputation.

Pluto has five moons. The nearest, Charon, named after the ferryman who took souls across the River Styx, is large and moves so close to its host planet that it gives the effect of a double planet rather than a planet with a satellite. This relationship is reminiscent of Hades's rulership of the underworld with Persephone, where they were the only living beings among the shades of the dead.

One year on Pluto around the sun equals 248 Earth years, and Pluto's orbit is unusual and erratic, both elliptical and tilted. It can move as far away from the Sun as 49.3 AU (astronomical units) and as close as 30 AU (4.5 to 7.3 billion kilometers and 2.8 to 4.6 billion miles), sometimes nearing the sun enough to melt some of its surface ice and leave comet-like trails of evaporated atmosphere. As it moves through the astrological constellations, its length of stay in each sign varies between twelve and thirty-two years.

In Your Natal Chart

The position of Pluto in your natal chart indicates how you deal with the experiences of symbolic death, regeneration, rebirth, renewal, and transformation. Although not related specifically to physical death, it reflects how we are affected by the endings of cycles in our lives and how we elevate ourselves to start afresh. The symbol of the phoenix rising from the ashes is appropriate to

Pluto. It represents the death of the old self in the fires of purification and initiation and the fresh flight of the new, elevated self that emerges triumphantly from the ashes of the past. Just as the snake must shed its old, tight skin as it grows, so does Pluto mark the sacred passages that lead to self-knowledge.

Because Pluto moves slowly in comparison to Earth time, its effect on the astrological signs is felt as generational rather than personal. Hades's rulership of the collective unconscious is reflected through the movement of Pluto through the Sun signs, an influence that ripples out through each generation and is felt as nearly seismic shifts in worldview.

Pluto's position in the houses of the natal chart reveals the areas of life in which the facilities for regeneration and transformation are at their most powerful. Pluto in the second house, for instance, reveals the ability to generate riches and a drive to accumulate wealth. In the seventh house, the planet indicates tremendous life-changes arising through relationships and a penetrating ability to understand the minds of others.

Because of Hades' position as both god of the underworld and the underworld as a place, Pluto in the natal chart is also concerned with conscious willpower and tendencies toward the exploration of hidden meanings. This search leads to a desire for self-knowledge through plumbing the depths of the psyche and through the occult, such as esoteric sciences and communion with the dead. When aspects are challenging, it can create morbidity, depression, emotional frigidity, and a preoccupation with the darker side of life. Issues of control and domination are predominant with challenging aspects, as the willpower is strong and is driven to assert itself over others.

When positively aspected, Pluto brings a strength of will that can overcome even apparently insurmountable obstacles. Because

there is no fear of death, the person has courage to take calculated risks; death is viewed as a natural element in the cycles of
life. Whereas Ares through the planet Mars is courageous to the
point of foolhardiness, Pluto is steel-willed and coldly determined
to win through. The talent for regeneration bestowed through
positive aspects to Pluto manifest as the ability to rise from blows
that seem impossible to survive and to use traumatic experiences
as stepping-stones to growth.

A strong Pluto engenders an intense desire to explore regions
where none have gone before, particularly those of the mind.
Psychology, investigations into human nature, and a fascination
with the occult are all elements of the Plutonian nature due to the
inner terrain that becomes accessible.

The Hades/Pluto connection carries connotations of associations with death, and so the position of Pluto can indicate money
or possessions that are gained through inheritances. Taxes are
another aspect of Pluto. Your ability to acquire and accumulate
wealth is also revealed through the area of the chart that Pluto is
situated in.

When Pluto is prominent in the natal chart, the eyes have a
compelling, hypnotic quality. The intensity in the gaze can make
some people feel uncomfortable because it appears that the individual can see through them, glimpsing underlying thoughts and
motivations. Similarly, the Plutonian gaze can also be extraordi-
narily compelling.

Rulership of Pluto

Pluto rules the astrological sign Scorpio and is symbolized by the
scorpion and the eagle. With its power to instill fear and its lethal
sting, the scorpion represents connection with the shadow aspect
of the underworld and death. The eagle symbolizes the ability of

the self to regenerate, to allow the mind to fly free and soar high above in order to see from a unique and far-sighted perspective. With its potential for plumbing the depths and attaining dizzying heights, the dual nature of this sign is part of Scorpio's mystery.

This astrological sign is viewed as the most powerful in the zodiac. Ruled by Pluto with a deep connection to the underworld of the unconscious mind and co-ruled by Mars with the Arian drive and the double dose of willpower bequeathed by both planets, these archetypes are both forces to be reckoned with. Added to this is the exaltation of Ouranos in Scorpio with its attendant insights and magnetic electrical charges of energy. Through Scorpio's contained forces, the potential for transformation is awe-inspiring.

Because of the links with desire, death, and rebirth, there are powerful sexual impulses that can lead to strong romantic attachments and possessiveness. As in the story of Hades and Persephone, the Scorpionic nature is driven by an urge to conquer the object of desire. The symbolic relationship between sex and death, with its connotations of merging into unity and release, is strongly felt in Scorpios and this drive can be acted out physically or transmuted into an overwhelming need to explore the secrets of life; to discover who we are and why we are here. This can be channeled through mystical experiences or research, or through the esoteric sciences.

The current quest in quantum physics to discover the Holy Grail of purpose in life is strongly influenced by Scorpio and Pluto. The deeper the sciences delve into the subatomic world, the realms of Hades, the more mysterious the findings become. What was once viewed as the smallest component of the universe, the atom, has proved to be yet another universe, with ever more subtle inhabitants. As this journey moves further into the complexities of inner space, the jewels that come to light become increasingly more exhilarating and intriguing because each discovery opens up new and astonishing realms that each appear to contain a consciousness of their own. As with the treasures hidden in the earth, careful digging is necessary before their secrets can be excavated and deciphered.

Scorpio nature is immensely resourceful and, due to its fixed nature, has a tremendous staying power. "Never say die" is the Scorpio motto, and people who are strongly influenced by this sign are determined to achieve their goals through a combination of strength of will and a refusal to give up. Superficiality is anathema to Scorpios, as they are impelled by an overwhelming urge to dig deep below the surface and uncover the reality of any situation they encounter. This strength enables them to battle against all odds and to use their secretive nature as a cloak that both protects them and prevents others from knowing them too intimately.

Although they refuse to admit weakness in themselves and strive to overcome shortcomings, the Scorpio's understanding of the underlying motivations in human nature makes them thoughtful and compassionate when they see other people struggling. They will endeavor to help others as long as a bargain is struck in which the other party is also willing to help themselves. They have little patience or tolerance for those who wish to be carried without contributing to the responsibility of self-help.

Diplomacy is not a Scorpio virtue, and they will remain silent rather than utter an untruth. What matters is the essence that lies at the core of experience; the understanding and insights that can be gained, and the effects that these will have in the long term.

Part 2
The Asteroids

Our solar system's main asteroid belt is located between Mars and Jupiter. It contains between 1.1 and 1.9 million asteroids that measure more than 0.6 miles (a kilometer) across, with millions more smaller ones. The largest is Ceres, with a diameter of 630 miles (1,000 kilometers). The brightest is Vesta, whose molten core once erupted through volcanoes and spilled lava across its surface.

The asteroids came into being early in the formation of the solar system. Newly born Jupiter's gravity was so strong that it prevented nearby planets from fully forming, and these collided with each other and broke into pieces of space rubble that traveled through a region about 140 million miles across (over 225 million kilometers).

The asteroids were discovered in around 1800, and the first four to be seen were named Ceres, Pallas Athene, Juno, and Vesta, after the Roman goddesses. Respectively, their Greek equivalents were Demeter, Athena, Hera, and Hestia. Chiron was discovered later, in 1977, generating much excitement. Situated between Saturn and Ouranos, it was first thought to be a planet. But when a coma (a trail of gas and dust) became visible in its wake, Chiron was demoted to a comet with possibilities of being an asteroid. Nowadays it is more frequently known as a planetoid, a small planet that measures 120 miles (190 kilometers) across with a fifty-one-year orbit around the sun.

The geological properties of the asteroids are similar to those of planets with chemical traces left behind by reactions that took place within them in the distant past.

If the natal chart is to be interpreted fully, it needs to include the asteroids and Chiron. The asteroids named after goddesses represent the female archetypes missing in the traditional view, and Chiron represents the male aspect of wisdom and healing. Without them, the feminine is allocated only to the roles of virginal mother (the Moon, Artemis) and lover (Venus/Aphrodite). This limitation does not allow balance within the female psyche or the inner feminine of the male psyche. When included, the wife (Juno/Hera), the earth mother (Ceres/Demeter), the warlike active thinker (Pallas Athene/Athena), and the light-bearer and mystic (Vesta/Hestia) enable a rounded, more holistic view. Chiron fulfills the role of wise and benevolent teacher and healer, the centaur tutor to the gods and heroes, whose skills in medicine, music, hunting, and warfare were highly respected.

Rulership of the asteroids is a subject still frequently under debate. Signs such as Virgo, which shares Mercury with Gemini, and Scorpio, which has Mars and Pluto as rulers, hold particularly strong resonances with more than one asteroid. The characteristics of the astrological signs often carry connections with several archetypes depending on which elements are expressed. Human nature is complex, and the personalities of the deities reflect this. You can liken this to the function of a violin string that contains the potential for many notes, and that reverberates specific notes depending on where and how pressure is applied to it.

In the symphony of the natal chart, the voices of the asteroids also have their places. If we listen to them and allow them to blend their subtle harmonies with the rest, we can attain increased psychological balance and a clearer view of our purpose.

Chapter Twelve

Chiron

Chiron rules Chiron, Virgo, Sagittarius, and the sixth and ninth houses.

The essential nature of Chiron is wisdom through experience. The suffering that this god endured acted as a spur to innovation, to compassion and altruism, to sacrifice, and ultimately to healing and rebirth.

As the wounded healer, Chiron is the symbol of courage, determination, and unselfishness. Able to ease the suffering of others yet helpless to cure himself, his journey led him to discover that only through releasing and relinquishing can the spirit truly be free to experience its immortality.

The archetype of the healer manifests through Chiron as the recognition that matter and energy are inextricably interconnected. He reminds us that the source of healing must be sought before progression can be made. As with the homeopathic principle of "like cures like," Chiron reminds us that only through identifying, recognizing, and accepting our inner wounds can we find true healing.

The Birth of Chiron

Chiron was the son of Kronos and Philyra and was conceived before Zeus challenged his father and rescued his siblings. In her flight from Kronos, Philyra turned herself into a horse to get away swiftly, but Kronos transformed himself into a stallion to catch up with and mate with her. The result of their union was Chiron, whose physiology was that of a centaur: half-man, half-horse.

Appalled at the sight of the creature she had birthed, Philyra abandoned him and begged the gods to release her from her mortal form. Her pleas were answered—she was turned into a linden tree whose healing blossoms could be used to promote sleep, a symbol of her refusal to "wake up" to the situation she found herself in.

Chiron became renowned for his wisdom and his skills in medicine, the arts, divination, hunting, and warfare. Whereas the other centaurs were fond of rough pursuits and debauchery, Chiron made his home in a cave in Thessaly and followed a higher path. He taught Apollo to play the lyre he had won from Hermes, and he became tutor to Apollo's son, Asclepius, passing on his knowledge of healing. When Asclepius raised a mortal from the dead, Hades complained to Zeus, fearing that the underworld would lose its population, resulting in Zeus killing Asclepius with a thunderbolt.

Chiron mentored other heroes, including Achilles and Jason, from whom they learned many of their skills. When Chiron died, Zeus placed him in the heavens as the constellation Centaurus.

Personality Traits

Chiron was rejected by both of his parents. Philyra found his appearance abhorrent, and Kronos was too busy trying to keep his power from being taken by his children with Rhea. Because of this, Chiron grew up alone and unloved, isolated from those he needed to feel close to. His energy was channeled into learning the skills that he would eventually teach, and his intelligence and compassion—both born of suffering—marked him as an inspired and inspiring counselor, healer and tutor, and devoted friend.

His wisdom was said to be a gift from Athena, bequeathed when she laid her hand on his forehead. He was generous with his knowledge, and gods and mortals benefited equally from it. All who came to him for healing or tuition found themselves deeply touched. He was greatly loved for his gentle spirit and unselfishness as well as for his skills, but he was set apart by his differences from his fellow centaurs and from mortals and gods.

Chiron's understanding of herb lore was profound, and he continually discovered and developed new ways in which to facilitate the healing process. Yet when these skills were needed for himself, he could not bring about the cure he sought. It is this facet of Chiron that is most strongly emphasized in his archetypal and astrological resonances.

The Wounded Healer

There are two wounds associated with Chiron. The first was emotional, a result of the rejection he suffered from both parents. The second was physical and accidental.

Chiron was inflicted with a terrible wound that poisoned him and made him suffer greatly. Because he was immortal, he could not die, much as he wished to release himself from the painful prison that his body became. Ultimately, it was an altruistic act that set him free and allowed him to die.

There are several versions of the story of how Chiron received his bodily wound. In one, he was accidentally struck by a spear that left a wound that would not heal. In another, a poisoned arrow he was removing from an injured centaur pricked him. A third story tells how Heracles accidentally wounded him in battle. The wound festered and caused him tremendous agony that he could not escape from, try as he might. His pain drove him to find ever more effective ways of healing the sick that worked on others, yet he was immune to everything that he used on himself. The knowledge of his immortality and the horror of living through eternity in constant pain led him to decide to die by offering himself in place of Prometheus, who had been cast out by the gods.

Prometheus was the son of the titan Iapetus, one of the early gods. He took Zeus's side when Zeus overthrew his father but fell out of favor with him because of his love for mortals, something Zeus considered beneath his station. Zeus had fire but kept it hidden, thinking it too potent to be used by others, but Prometheus stole it and gave it to mortals. In his fury, Zeus sent Prometheus to Tartarus, the realm of the underworld where he was chained to a rock and left to suffer eternal torment. Each day an eagle tore out his liver, and each night it grew whole again to be repeated day after day. Trapped there, abandoned by his kin, it seemed that there would be no end to his suffering, until Chiron interceded. He begged to be permitted to take the place of Prometheus. Zeus agreed, Prometheus was released, and Chiron was chained to the rock. After nine days he died, and Zeus placed him in the heavens as the constellation Centaurus.

Relationships

Chiron joined the centaurs in some of their revelries but avoided becoming involved in their lustiness, preferring to live quietly in his cave on Mount Pelion in Thessaly. Nevertheless, he was greatly loved and inspired respect through his qualities of kindness and generosity. As tutor to gods and mortals, he gave of himself unstintingly and passed on whichever skills were sought, whether in medicine and healing, or in the skills of warfare.

Athena was fond of Chiron to the extent of bestowing one of her gifts on him, adding to his innate wisdom. Apollo also thought highly of him; in some stories, he became Chiron's benefactor and guardian after being abandoned by his parents, though this tale is rather unlikely chronologically, as Chiron was born before Zeus overthrew Kronos and Apollo was one of Zeus's sons.

There was no significant lover in Chiron's life. His role as a priestlike figure to the centaurs and as a being whose focus was on the needs of others meant that his own were somewhat neglected. His sense of self was damaged through his rejection by his parents, and his theme carries an underlying sadness despite willingness to give of himself to others. The relationships he did engage in were ones in which he was very much the giver rather than the receiver. As the wise one, tutor, healer, astrologer, and sage, his time and energy were devoted to the well-being of all who entered his sphere.

Siblings

Chiron had no full-blood siblings, though the children of Kronos were his half-brothers and sisters. His heritage was tightly bound to the titans, the primal nature gods and goddesses who brought all manner of strange creatures to birth. Although he was unlike his relatives, his relationships with them were benign; his altruistic nature made him pleasant to those who sought him out.

Archetypal Resonance

Chiron as an archetype embodies the shaman, the wounded healer and teacher who links body, mind, and spirit and who catalyzes healing in those around him as a result of his skills and actions.

The suffering Chiron endured was not of his own creation—neither his abandonment by his parents that left an internal emotional wound nor the physical wound that came later and caused continual pain. But these experiences led him to seek new methods of healing. Chiron's wounds became a blueprint for his archetypal resonance because both stemmed from trust; the trust of a child that his parents would love and care for him and the trust as a healer that good would come about through helping others. Chiron's wounds were healed through making the ultimate sacrifice—himself—and that surrender led him to a state of healing and wholeness.

As half-man and half-horse, Chiron embodies the connection between the intellectual, philosophical, conscious mind and the instinctual, unconscious mind. A synthesis between these is a necessary prerequisite for wisdom. Without instinct, philosophizing is purely cerebral, detached from the nitty-gritty of everyday life. The combination of both of these elements creates a profound search for, and understanding of, what gives meaning to our lives.

Chiron's inability to heal himself is reflected in life through areas in which we can be useful to others through recognizing and coming to terms with our own inner wounds. Despite his pain, he refused to give up or give in; instead, it spurred him on to discover new forms of healing that could benefit others. His wounds prompted him to reach out and use his skills to their fullest to be of service to others in need. This archetype is prominent in people whose suffering, either through loss or illness, motivates them to train in counseling or some form of healing or set up organizations and support groups that offer help and an exchange of information.

In one of the versions of Chiron's wounding, the cause was an arrow shot by Heracles that accidentally struck Chiron, an act with tremendous significance in Chiron's ultimate healing and subsequent placement in the heavens, for it was Heracles who interceded on Chiron's behalf and persuaded Zeus to allow Chiron to take Prometheus's place in Tartarus. Their substitution shows us that the cause of the initial wound ultimately provides the facility for healing to take place. The wound itself was not healed, but the cause—in this case, the perpetrator—was eventually the means by which release from pain was accomplished.

An element of sacrifice is clear in Chiron's archetypal resonance. His physical wound was a result of his intercession on others' behalf. He was willing to risk all in order to be of service. His solution to his own suffering was to relieve the agony of Prometheus by taking his place—to save a life through offering up his own life. Through this act he attained release and regained the state of immortality. When we take action on behalf of others with no thought for what might happen to ourselves, we are connecting with Chiron. When we face a choice in which a sacrifice must be made in order to attain our goal, Chiron's voice can be heard within the psyche. Ultimately, the path we take through our decisions leads to the higher good.

In Your Natal Chart

The position of Chiron in the natal chart reveals where we carry an inner wound that has the potential to become our greatest gift. Discovery of this gift prompts a search for healing that facilitates wholeness within ourselves and enables us to reach out to others and touch others deeply. Chiron's astronomical position between Saturn and Ouranos represents the bridge between the oppression of inner needs that are not being met and the unusual and unexpected solution that leads to freedom and release.

The path to healing mapped out in Chiron's position in the natal chart is gained through acceptance. Wherever Chiron rests represents the focus for our feelings of rejection or pain at the hands of others. Chiron's unique relationship with gods and mortals and his abilities as a wise one and teacher came about in part because of his underlying loneliness. His early rejection created a sense of isolation, of not belonging. He avoided the coarse behavior of the other centaurs yet was not mortal. His place was that of intermediary where he used his considerable gifts born of suffering to help others. In return, he was blessed with great wisdom that gave him a status that gods and mortals both recognized.

Wounds are an aspect of life. We cannot pass through life unscathed, because the experience of feeling opens up avenues to rejection and pain. Yet through rejection and pain we become compassionate, empathic, and sympathetic. Our own suffering creates an ability to understand others and use our resources to be of help.

Challenging aspects to Chiron indicate blocks that stand in the way of healing that can drain the energy through emotional experiences of despair and hopelessness and a lack of self-acceptance. When challenged, manifesting Chiron's positive aspects is more challenging and difficult to work with. Yet these blocks themselves are often the key to resolution, just as Chiron's wound impelled him to discover more about healing methods. There can be a perception of the self as either the wounded victim or the perpetrator of wounds inflicted on others if no attempts are made to examine the causes of these attitudes and find a way to work constructively with them.

Positive aspects to Chiron reveal the forces that can be accessed through building a bridge between the instinctual mind and the spiritual self. These indicate the potential to grow through developing the capacity for nurturing and accumulating wisdom.

Rulership of Chiron

There is much debate between astrologers over which sign is ruled by Chiron. On one side of the arena stands Sagittarius, the centaur with his bow and arrow who expresses himself philosophically and spiritually. The Sagittarian nature accords with Chiron's quality of active intelligence that leads the native with a desire to pass on their gifts to others through teaching what they know. In his rulership of Sagittarius, Chiron carries the instrument associated with his own wound (the arrow) and must use his insight and intelligence to discover how healing can be facilitated.

The Sagittarian qualities of aloofness and looking down from above coupled with an innate friendliness, honesty, and openness resonate strongly with Chiron's demeanor, as does this sign's quest for knowledge and truth.

Virgo also claims the right to rulership of Chiron and holds some convincing arguments in their favor, chiefly aspects of healing, service, and sacrifice that Chiron embodies. Virgo's need to be of service to others further accentuates the Virgo impulse toward maintaining inner and outer health through exploring holistic forms of healing. The Virgoan intellect, purity, and self-effacing qualities, the Virgo's diffidence about putting themselves forward, and their willingness to sacrifice their own needs in order to fulfil those of others are qualities that resonate strongly with Chiron.

The Sagittarian intellect is geared toward the accumulation of knowledge through study and education and formal bodies of learning such as colleges and universities. The Virgoan intelligence is more earthy; wisdom is sought and gained through direct experience in the "university of life," itself closer to the manner in which Chiron discovered and then honed and developed his skills through experimentation.

When Chiron was first discovered, Virgoans heaved a sigh of relief and staked their claim. It seemed that their ruling planet had appeared at last and could work alongside Mercury, allowing the sign's qualities fuller expression and realization. As the debate continues over which sign (if not both) Chiron truly rules, only time—of which Chiron as offspring of Kronos is the son—will allow evidence for each astrological sign's rulership to be clarified.

Chapter Thirteen

Ceres — Demeter

Demeter/Ceres rules Ceres, Cancer, Virgo, and the fourth and sixth houses.

As the embodiment of the earth mother, Demeter is defined through her relationship with her daughter, Persephone, and with the land. Her fertility is expressed through both. An earth mother is one who nurtures her offspring, surrounds them with love and support, and protects them from harm. Yet children grow up and leave home, and the earth mother must then find other outlets for this fecund energy, lest they pine away in the absence of their children like Demeter.

Demeter's focus is purely upon her daughter. Without Persephone, there is no channel for joy or creativity, and winter descends upon the emotional landscape. Yet within each winter the seeds sleep, awaiting the warm touch of springtime.

The Birth of Demeter

As a daughter of Kronos and Rhea, Demeter's father swallowed her at birth and was later retrieved when Zeus defeated Kronos and administered a powerful herbal emetic. Whereas her brothers divided the realms of the sky, sea, and underworld between them, Demeter became goddess of the earth and all growing things.

Her symbol was grain, specifically corn. It was she who woke the earth and encouraged it to produce, and she was kind and sympathetic toward mortals who in turn revered her as the source of all nourishment. Demeter taught mortals how to grow and harvest crops to feed themselves and their livestock, and she was associated with abundance and fertility. As goddess of fecundity, she was depicted carrying a sheaf of grain and poppies; the wheat a symbol of the earth's bounty and poppies to symbolize death and rebirth.

As devoted earth mother, Demeter's story is inextricably linked with Persephone's, her daughter by Zeus. Her close relationship with her daughter was the cause of the seasons, and the Eleusinian rites that were performed each year enacted the story of mother and daughter's love for each other, the loss that both were subjected to, and their eventual reconciliation.

Persephone and Demeter

Persephone was a beautiful young woman who was devoted to her mother, who in turn loved her beyond all else. The two were inseparable, and although Persephone had many suitors, she chose to remain single and stay by her mother's side. Lovely in both appearance and temperament, malleable and acquiescent, Persephone was the embodiment of the innocent maiden—untouched, pure of spirit, no thought of fear or danger.

While she strolled with her maidens through the Nysian fields, plucking flowers for her mother, she strayed from Demeter's sight, unaware that Hades was observing her, having fallen in love with her. Determined to have her as his wife and lacking the finesse of her other suitors, Hades burst forth from the earth in his chariot drawn by black horses, swept Persephone away, and deaf to her screams for help, took her with him into the underworld to make her his bride.

Zeus witnessed his daughter's abduction but believed it was time she married and considered Hades to be a worthy husband for her, thus ignoring her cries and allowing Hades to take her. The earth that had opened to allow Hades to appear closed behind them, and they vanished.

When Demeter discovered that Persephone had disappeared, she searched the earth for her, crying out her daughter's name. She refused to eat or sleep and tore her clothes to rags and covered herself in dirt. Zeus turned away from Demeter's pleas for him to bring her daughter back; in anguish, Demeter left Olympus and wandered the earth as a wizened beggar woman. Much later, attempts were made to rescue Persephone. Theseus and Pirithous made their way into the underworld undetected, planning to find Persephone and bring her home. However, Hades caught them and imprisoned them in chains that made them forget who they were and why they were there.

Demeter's grief was so great that she prevented the earth from yielding its bounty. Winter came, the ground turned cold and hard, and nothing grew. The mortals she loved and cared for who relied on her for nourishment starved and froze until they pleaded with Zeus to intervene in desperation. Realizing that soon there would be no one to make sacrifices to him, Zeus commanded Demeter to appear before him. She refused. Zeus admitted defeat and sent Hermes to the underworld to fetch Persephone and return her to her mother.

When Hermes found her, she was seated beside Hades, sobbing. She had refused all food and drink and was in a state of deep depression. Hades agreed to set his wife free but only on condition that she first eat some pomegranate seeds. Unaware that this would bind her to him forever, Persephone took and ate a few, and Hermes escorted her back to Eleusis.

Demeter was so ecstatic at the sight of her daughter that the earth warmed and spring came. Plants, crops, and flowers burst forth, and the earth was bountiful once more. But when she discovered that Persephone had eaten the pomegranate seeds, she realized that her daughter was hers on loan only. If food or drink was taken in the underworld, a pact was made that ensured only a temporary stay away from that realm. The earth immediately grew cold once again.

Finally, a compromise was reached: Persephone would spend a portion of each year with her mother and a portion with Hades in the underworld. The number of seeds that she had eaten were to determine the number of months that she must spend with Hades. Demeter had no choice but to reluctantly agree.

When Persephone made her annual journey to the underworld, Demeter marked her period of mourning by withdrawing her life-giving energy from the earth, the relationship between mother and daughter determining the seasons. Springtime comes with Persephone's joyful return to her mother, the summer shows the warmth of their mutual love, autumn marks the decline as they prepare to be parted, and winter comes when Persephone leaves Demeter to make her journey back to the underworld.

Personality Traits

Demeter is the archetype of the devoted mother who does all she can to protect her offspring from harm in a love that is all-encompassing. The glow of her warmth radiates out to touch all of humanity, who benefit from her generosity, just as a new mother holding her child experiences a rush of love and compassion that becomes universal rather than merely personal.

As earth goddess, Demeter was the embodiment of abundance. She taught mortals the arts of agriculture, and her benevolence and fertility were a source of boundless nourishment to all. In fact, our word "cereal" stems from her Roman name, Ceres, and one of her symbols, the cornucopia has long signified the rich harvest of the earth's gifts.

Demeter's child was of primary importance to her. When Persephone was abducted, Demeter's grief was so overwhelming that the earth itself became barren. The love she bore for mortals was eclipsed under the weight of her despair at losing her daughter. She was the embodiment of maternal love and protectiveness at its most powerful, and her rage at Hades's abduction and Zeus's withdrawal from the situation made her immune to the pleas of the starving mortals who had for so long been enfolded in her embrace and the gods who each brought gifts to her to attempt to persuade her to change her mind.

However, she was not fully closed to others even in her distraught state. When she realized that Persephone was in the underworld, she disguised herself as an old woman and traveled to Eleusis. Taken in by Demeter's appearance, Queen Metanira took her on as nursemaid to her baby son, Demophon.

The child grew strong thanks to Demeter's nurturing, and she decided to bestow on him the gift of immortality. Each night she placed him in the fire and each day she fed him ambrosia, the food of the gods. But one night, Queen Metanira entered the chamber to see Demeter apparently about to kill her son, aghast. Demeter then revealed her true nature and demanded that a temple dedicated to her should be built. Eleusis later became the site where the Eleusinian rites were held each year.

Demeter's willingness to give immortality to a mortal child illustrates how the mothering instinct cannot be quashed, even in times of great stress and grief. Her desire to care for and protect her daughter extended to the human child in her care.

Relationships

Demeter's first relationship was with her parents. Unlike her brothers, who claimed their kingdoms and immediately left to go rule them, Demeter was close to her mother, Rhea, and carried on the heritage of earth goddess that had passed through the female line starting with Gaia. All these goddesses had great pain inflicted on them by their consorts and rebelled against them in order to protect their children. Gaia plotted against Ouranos. Rhea enlisted the advice of Gaia and Ouranos to prevent Kronos from swallowing any more of his children, and Demeter's helplessness in the wake of Zeus's uncaring attitude toward Persephone led to the onset of winter on Earth. The relationships of these three goddesses with the father-figure were strained and marred by abuse, in turn affecting their choice of mate and who would receive their affections.

Zeus's and Demeter's coupling occurred before Zeus married Hera, which saved her from being subjected to Hera's jealous fury, unlike the many who came after her.

Demeter had no desire for other relationships after Persephone's birth. Her daughter received the full focus of Demeter's love, a love that was so intense that it spilled over to engulf the earth and all living things.

Sibling Rivalry

The most noteworthy relationships between Demeter and her siblings were those with Zeus and Hades. Zeus was her first and only lover and father of her daughter. Hades was the abductor and husband of Persephone. Until that event occurred, Demeter and Zeus had maintained a cordial though somewhat detached relationship. She loved her daughter so dearly that she viewed the past relationship as the means through which she had attained her heart's desire. As Hades was rarely seen outside the underworld, it was only when he deprived Demeter of Persephone's presence that he reentered her consciousness.

Demeter's grief as well as her rage toward both of her brothers was immense. She withdrew into herself and closed the life-supporting benevolence that had nurtured those on Earth. Even as king of the gods, Zeus could not force or persuade Demeter to make the earth fertile again.

Although eventually reconciled with her daughter, Demeter had to agree to share her with Hades. The pomegranate seeds Persephone had eaten bound her to her husband and thus his realm. Demeter showed her mettle by refusing to give up the fight for her daughter but had no choice but to honor the agreement. All the same, she was powerful enough to state her own terms. While Persephone was absent each year, winter would hold the earth in its cold embrace.

Archetypal Resonance

Demeter as an archetype embodies all-encompassing mother-love, the deep inner drive to give birth and nurture and protect one's young from harm. The element within the psyche that yearns to look after others is expressed through maternal instincts that seek any available avenue of expression. It can manifest as a literal, physical experience of motherhood or in "motherly" behavior that others seek and turn to for support and tender loving care.

One aspect that marks the Demeter archetype shows in situations where the needs of the children, friends, or receivers of care take precedence over the needs and wishes of the husband or partner, which can engender resentment. The benevolent side of Demeter is prominent in all those who radiate acceptance and unconditional love. Whether they are literal or symbolic mothers, there is a fertile quality that has the effect of encouraging growth and development of self-esteem in those around them.

The powerful elements in the story of Demeter and Persephone illustrate different aspects of this archetype. She is a devoted mother who keeps her child close to her and who inspires total love and trust in return, but this protectiveness can be stifling if overdone. One of the tasks of motherhood is to encourage the child to learn independence and autonomy in a safe space. Each step toward this gradually opens up new vistas until the child is grown and has the self-confidence to participate in the adult world. Demeter's devotion to Persephone was such that the child remained a child, even when she came of marriageable age. She was so strongly attached to her mother that their relationship was intense and self-perpetuating; all others were viewed as insignificant or unnecessary. This is not a healthy one, and what transpired with Hades created a sudden, brutal wrench for both mother and daughter that forced Persephone to enter the adult world and Demeter to eventually accept that her daughter was now a woman *and* her child.

On the day Persephone was abducted, she had strayed out of her mother's sight and was gathering flowers in a meadow. Her innocence and ignorance of the world beyond her tightly-knit relationship with Demeter was total. Hades emerging from the earth to carry her away is the shock that accompanies the end of childhood if no preparations have been made. Persephone was unprepared due to her closeness to Demeter, and the separation sent her into a state of depression that accentuated her passivity.

We cannot live out our adult lives under the protective umbrellas of our mothers even should we wish to, because the urge toward growth and autonomy is instinctual. Persephone's momentary straying beyond Demeter's influence created the opportunity for Hades to rush in and capture her. Welcome as it was, Demeter's control over Persephone was substituted for that of Hades.

Another element in the story of Demeter and Persephone is the anguish of the mother who has lost her child. The process of mourning cuts off all access to the flow of the life force, as when Demeter brought winter to the land. Only when a focus emerges for the nurturing energy can healing begin, as with Demeter and baby Demophon. Those with a strong Demeter connection can experience a similar sense of loss of purpose and depression when children grow up and leave home.

The archetype's shadow aspect comes to the fore when the flow of mutual love is blocked. Demeter withdrew her fertile nature from the earth, leaving the mortals, animals, flora, and fauna in the precarious position of struggling to survive. When the goddess's darker elements come to the fore, the Demeter archetype can be experienced as a withdrawal of love, nurturing, and support; the destructive "dark mother" who is too locked into her own feelings to be aware of those of others.

The fullest expression of the Demeter archetype lies in the will and the ability to love deeply, protect, nurture, and foster a sense of self. The greatest challenge comes from learning to let go, accepting the knowledge that love includes the need to allow loved ones the freedom to live independent lives. When we accept it, the sense of security innate to this bond ensures that those let go will always return—as mature adults rather than as eternal children.

In Your Natal Chart

The position of the asteroid Ceres in the natal chart reveals how we experience and work with issues of nurturing and being nurtured. The relationship with the mother can be more clearly defined and understood as can that of our own attitudes toward parenting. The sign Ceres is found in acts as a lens for our perception of needs, showing whether we feel loved and cherished and if the bond with the mother has been loving, suffocating, toxic, or ambiguous.

Our attitudes toward our children (whether of the body or the mind) are reflected in the whatever astrological sign Ceres rests in, indicating whether we will be nurturing, detached, or possessive. Attitudes around childcare and relationships are also signified, along with issues of sexuality. If Ceres is prominent in the natal chart, the male in a woman's life can feel insignificant compared to the children. If the voice of Ceres is balanced by other archetypal voices, such as Venus/Aphrodite or Juno/Hera, then the relationships with children and partner are likely to be more balanced and constructive. The nurturing power of Ceres can then be channeled into the creation of a nucleus of love and warmth that has a vitalizing effect on everyone who enters its sphere.

Ceres in the houses indicates how we go about ensuring that our emotional and physical needs are nurtured. Through the house position, we see our willingness and ability to seek out the experiences we need in order to foster a sense of self-love as well as the areas of experience that will provide the outlet for it.

Aspects to Ceres indicate whether our ability to nurture and accept nurturing from others is free-flowing or blocked. Challenging aspects have the effect of either generating over-possessiveness that has an inhibiting effect on loved ones or conversely an inability to relate to and connect deeply with those around us. Positive aspects to Ceres reveal healthy, wholesome family relationships that generate a strong sense of self-worth and trust. There are feelings of abundance, and family life is viewed as fertile ground that encourages growth as it provides security.

Rulership of Ceres

The primary rulership of Ceres is in Cancer, with the strong maternal instinct of that sign connecting profoundly with the Ceres/Demeter archetype. Cancer's planetary ruler, the Moon, denotes life's tides, the ebb and flow of fertility through the menstrual cycle, and the attitudes toward mothering and nurturing. Cancer rules the breasts, the source of nourishment for infants. Ceres' rulership of this sign travels deeper into the blood and milk areas of maternity, whereas Artemis, the cool Moon goddess, manifests less as the physical mother and more as the protector of women in childbirth.

Ceres's qualities of deep attachment and unconditional love as well as her role as matrix of security are evident in the sign of the crab. Also prominent is the typically Cancerian retreat into a hard shell when hurt. Demeter's refusal to listen to others while she was grieving over the loss of Persephone and her chosen isolation from the world she loved (that depended on her), is markedly similar to the Cancerian response to emotional pain. The Cancerian gift of enveloping loved ones in a rosy cocoon of caring and sharing also applies to Ceres, not only with Persephone but also the mortals to whom she gave the earth's fertile abundance.

There are indisputable connections between the possessiveness of Cancerians and Ceres. Whether romantic or familial, relationships are so vital to the Cancerian psyche that well-being is strongly bound with the physical closeness of the loved one. The leash is often short and tightly held, as Cancerians tend to want their beloved to remain in the immediate vicinity: the mother who needs to know where her child is at every moment, even when that child is grown; the child who clings closely to the mother; the partner who needs the constant physical presence of their significant other—all exemplify the type of love that Demeter and Persephone shared. Often the break, when it comes (as it must, in order for the child to grow up) is sudden and traumatic.

Cancerians have a reputation for being good cooks. Food is important to them for physical nourishment, but it is also a means of giving and receiving love. When they feed others, they can express their innate nurturing capabilities physically and emotionally. Ceres's role as earth goddess, her gift of agriculture, and her qualities of nourishing and nurturing accord closely with the Cancerian nature.

Ceres is also connected to Virgo. The image of the goddess holding a sheaf of grain is very similar to pictorial representations of this sign. Virgos are less noted astrologically for their maternal instincts (though many do carry the role of earth mother well) because of their conventional reputation for purity and chastity. Yet the qualities inherent in nurturing others are pronounced in this sign. The Virgoan attention to the well-being of those around them, the focus on nourishment through careful attention to preparing food, and the element of service to others all resonate with the Ceres archetype. Yet in the case of Virgo, the focus on food is for the maintenance of health rather than as something emotional in nature.

Virgos need to feel that they can contribute in some way for the good of humanity, a quality that bears resemblance to Ceres's love of mortals. She chose to live among them, taught them agriculture, and was prepared to gift the baby Demophon with immortality, all to raise him to her spiritual level. The Virgoan nature strives to help others with no expectation of reward; as an earth sign, Virgo also has a strong connection with the processes of life and growth.

However, the Demeter-Persephone connection with its codependency and inability of either party to let go is more Cancerian. Although Ceres holds a resonance that sings through both Cancer and Virgo, it is in the sign of motherhood where her voice is heard most powerfully.

Chapter Fourteen

Juno — Hera

Hera/Juno rules Juno, Libra, Scorpio, and the seventh and eighth houses.

Hera is the embodiment of commitment. Despite the trials her husband Zeus inflicted on her, she held firm and refused to give up on their marriage. Her pride distanced her from the other Olympians, and her fury brought disaster to the lives of those who did not honor the sanctity of marriage.

Hera's integrity in holding to her principles was unshakeable within a family that viewed casual liaisons as the norm. Her willingness to repeatedly take her husband back was mirrored among the immortals only in the marriage of her rejected son, Hephaestus, to Aphrodite. Hera held to her beliefs despite formidable opposition because her sense of identity was closely bound with the position she held as wife of the leader of the gods.

The Birth of Hera

Like the other children of Kronos and Rhea, except for Zeus, Hera was swallowed by her father at birth. When she emerged from the belly of Kronos, she lived with

Oceanus and Tethys, titan children of Gaia and Ouranos, until Zeus, allied with the titans, overthrew his father. When Zeus took the throne and set the scene for the Olympian era to begin, Hera left her foster-carers and went to live on Olympus.

Her beauty was enchanting, and she was chaste, refusing to give herself to any man before marriage. After Zeus had indulged in affairs with others, including his sister Demeter, who bore him Persephone, his roving eye alighted on Hera and he pursued her. Hera, however, rebuffed him until Zeus turned himself into a cuckoo during a storm and nestled at her breast. Hera's sympathies were aroused, and when Zeus returned to his mortal form she agreed to be his consort on condition that he marry her. The marriage was initially happy until Zeus resumed his philandering to the mortification and fury of his wife—the goddess of marriage. She took revenge on Zeus's lovers rather than on her husband, which still did not deter goddesses, nymphs, and mortals from responding to his advances.

Hera bore associations with the Pagan Great Goddess, also known as the Triple Goddess of life and death. In ancient tales, the milk that flowed from her breast created the Milky Way galaxy. This connection filtered into the mythology of the Olympians, where Hera was considered queen of Heaven and her husband's equal.

Personality Traits

There are two distinct aspects to Hera's personality. The poet Homer took a very negative view of her and portrayed her as a vengeful, vindictive, henpecking wife who sniped at her husband and punished his paramours harshly. This characterization has tended to override Hera's positive qualities and has given her an unbalanced and unpleasant reputation.

Hera did wreak terrible vengeance on those who coupled with her husband. Leto, the mother of Artemis and Apollo, was forced to wander the earth in search of a place to give birth, because none dared risk Hera's wrath after coming to Leto's aid.

When Zeus seduced Callisto, who was a member of Artemis's forest nymphs, he disguised himself as Artemis in order to get close to her, and she bore him a son, Arcas. Later, when Hera found out, she changed Callisto into a bear and tried to trick Arcas into unknowingly slaying his mother. Before he could do so, Zeus intervened and transformed Arcas into a bear, too, then placed the mother and son in the heavens as Ursa Major and Ursa Minor, the bear constellations.

Hera's vindictive side stemmed from her view of marriage as sacred. Her sense of self was inextricably tied in with her role as wife and consort. Leaving Zeus permanently was unthinkable to her, although on several occasions she fled from Olympus and retreated within herself until her emotional wounds had time to heal. Then she would return, there would be another brief honeymoon period, and Zeus would resume his philandering—and so the cycle continued.

Her husband's affairs and his large brood of illegitimate children caused Hera great anguish. That Zeus could sully their relationship was hurtful and humiliating for her, yet she could not bring herself to make him suffer for his behavior. His children by other women were less fortunate.

Dionysus, the god of wine and ecstasy, was the son of Zeus and Semele, a Theban princess. The Romans called him Bacchus, and their rites carried out in his name were wild and orgiastic. His followers, the maenads, would enter into frenzied, ecstatic states that often culminated in debauchery and dismemberment. Hera tried several times to kill him and was successful in driving his foster-parents insane, but Dionysus proved too strong for her. Eventually he died at the hands of his frenzied maenads and his grave was placed at Delphi. For the months of the year while Apollo retreated to Hyperborea, Dionysus took charge of the Delphic Oracle.

Of the Greek heroes, the strongest was Heracles (known to the Romans as Hercules), son of Zeus and Alcmene. His mother had married King Amphitryon of Tiryns on condition that the marriage would take place after Amphitryon had taken revenge on her brothers' murderers. While the king was away carrying out his task, Zeus came to Alcmene disguised as her future husband and told her that the deed had been accomplished. She went into his arms willingly, and Heracles was conceived. When her husband returned, he found that Alcmene was under the illusion that he had already taken her virginity, and eventually the truth became known. The infant was given the name Heracles, "Hera's Glory." Zeus assumed that Hera would be flattered, but instead she was deeply insulted and outraged. She made every attempt within her power to destroy Heracles, ignoring Zeus's explanations as to why he had created this child. He knew there would be a battle between the gods and a race of giants, and he intended for his son to be a mortal of such strength that his opponents would be surely defeated.

For her part, Hera hated Heracles. She sent two snakes to kill the baby, but the infant slew them. Later, she caused him to go insane and murder his wife and three children. His remorse at what he had done led him to undertake the Twelve Labors, accomplishing feats considered to be beyond the power of any mortal. It was also Heracles who negotiated with Zeus for Chiron to take the place of Prometheus in Tartarus and be allowed to die and be reborn again as an immortal.

As a mother, Hera had none of the nurturing qualities of her sister, Demeter. When Zeus birthed Athena parthenogenically from his forehead, Hera retaliated by conceiving Hephaestus without the help of her husband. When the child was born with a club foot, Hera hurled him from Olympus to Earth, furious that he was not perfect. In another version of the story, Hephaestus remained with Hera until he took his mother's side during an argument between her and Zeus, and it was Zeus who angrily threw him from the heights of Olympus. Hephaestus later married Aphrodite, the only goddess (other than Hera) to enter wedlock, and he was subjected to a similar marital situation to Hera as his wife flaunted her unfaithfulness.

Ares was also a son of Zeus and Hera who disappointed his parents. He had none of the cool logic the gods respected, and both his parents disliked him intensely because they considered him to be impetuous, foolhardy, and bloodthirsty, blind as they were to his more appealing and attractive qualities. Zeus's and Hera's daughters, Hebe and Eileithyia, remained in the background of the Olympian pantheon.

Despite her indisputably dark side, Greeks worshiped Hera (and later in Rome as Juno) as the benevolent goddess of marriage, whose blessing could bestow sanctity and happiness on a couple. Three separate rituals were dedicated to her each year in her honor that preserved her association as the pre-Olympian Great Goddess, the triple goddess in her aspects of maiden, mother, and crone.

The celebration of the Maiden aspect was held in the springtime, the Mother aspect in summer, and the Crone in winter. Spring saw Hera as the virginal maiden, summer was the consummation of her marriage, and winter marked her season as the wise old crone, the widow who holds a direct connection with death.

The Sacred Marriage

The sacred marriage Hera represented was more than merely the physical union between man and woman, god and goddess in the eyes of the world. Hera's perception of marriage was the purity and sanctity of the coming together of the highest, most spiritual aspects of male and female, a combination that led to mystical experience. All levels of being were integrated—physical, emotional, mental, and spiritual. This sacred marriage embodied a true merging of souls and a uniting of opposites. The search for a soul-mate, the elusive "one," is the contemporary vision of access to Hera's most potent domain.

Hera's vision of marriage was a blissful state of union. Before wedding Zeus, she had lofty ideals about the joys and responsibilities it involved. To then discover that her husband held an entirely different view wherein he considered all women receptacles for his seed was a profoundly devastating experience for his idealistic wife. As violent and extreme as her responses were, perhaps they were also unsurprising.

Relationships

Hera had no relationships before marrying Zeus. She was an innocent maiden similar to Persephone, but whereas Persephone had no desire to leave her mother, Hera believed that marriage was the highest state that one could attain. She was not an earth mother like Rhea and had to contend with an infanticidal father like all the first-generation Olympians. As daughter to a nourishing mother and a father who was overthrown by his own son, she followed the pattern of entering an abusive relationship.

Zeus loved her but felt no desire or need to be faithful to her, despite her obvious rage and anguish each time she discovered the presence of another paramour. She left him several times and wandered the earth, hiding the shame she felt when she faced the sly glances of the other Olympians. But each time she returned because she could not imagine her place as anywhere but at her husband's side. Where Zeus was concerned, she was the epitome of faithfulness, loyalty, and devotion.

Sibling Rivalry

Hera was sensitive to her situation as Zeus's first lady and consort, but his casual attitude toward her was a source of her public humiliation. She was set apart by virtue of her marriage, and her vengeance on those who lay with her husband was so terrifying that other goddesses avoided her.

She was not close to her siblings and had no confidants. She had a competitive streak and her beauty was a source of pride to her. The Trojan War was sparked by a contest between Hera, Aphrodite, and Athena over who was the loveliest. They chose Paris, son of the king of Troy, to award a golden apple to the most beautiful of the three goddesses, and each tried to bribe him in order to gain his favor. Hera offered Paris rulership over the lands of Asia, Athena offered him victory in war, and Aphrodite offered him the love of the most beautiful woman in the world. Paris awarded the golden apple to Aphrodite, but the beautiful woman in question was Helen, who was married to King Menelaus of Greece. The war that ensued between Greece and Troy after Paris and Helen eloped ended after ten years with Troy's defeat.

Archetypal Resonance

Hera as an archetype embodies the qualities of loyalty and commitment in a relationship experienced psychologically as the urge toward union with another. But whereas Aphrodite is the spark of attraction that provides the impulse toward romance and sensuality, union for Hera comes about through a deep need to have a significant other in life—no casual relationships here. This archetype manifests as the desire to be with one special person who will honor them in an enduring relationship. The young girl who is eager to have an engagement ring on her finger that she can show off to her friends and the young woman who rushes into marriage with high ideals and the expectations of a permanent happy ending are both typical expressions of the Hera archetype.

If a committed relationship is not forthcoming or there isn't one, the feelings of isolation and purposelessness can be intense and painful. Until comparatively recently, a woman defined herself and was defined by others through her husband. Feminism changed attitudes and enabled women to demonstrate that they could be happy and fulfilled whether single or married, but the Hera archetype still holds her place in the psyche. If her voice is strong, the urge toward a committed relationship becomes the overruling consideration.

This insistence can reach unhealthy and dangerous levels in abusive relationships, where others urge the woman to leave for her own or her children's protection and safety but she cannot bring herself to take a step out of the marital sphere. Like Hera, she cannot consider the abandonment of her husband, however difficult the marriage is.

The Hera archetype thrives in a healthy relationship based on mutual trust, respect, and the bond forged between partners that serve as an inspiration to all who know them. Together they appear to add up to more than the sum of the individuals, and the relationship itself takes on what amounts to a separate identity to those within it. When healthy, these relationships cast a radiance that shines through each partner. Hera fulfils her role as goddess of the sacred marriage and can bestow her highest blessings.

However, if her partner is unfaithful when the Hera archetype prevails, retribution can be swift and sometimes deadly. Crime of passion (in some countries still considered a justifiable act rather than as a punishable offense), is one manifestation of Hera's dark aspects. Her persecution of Zeus's lovers and their children was an extreme reaction reflected in less dramatic ways in contemporary society.

The Hera archetype's primary concern is the need to love and be loved, and this is exacerbated by the need to be publicly seen as cherished by a mate and to feel a certain status as a result. That said, Hera's voice needs to be heard alongside others if she is to be happy. The independence of Athena or Artemis can enable her to invest less of her self-perception in the person she is with, for Hera cannot feel complete without a mate who is willing to be a life-partner.

Her family is secondary to her husband, and this archetype may even resent the attention her children demand from her or be jealous of the love they receive from her spouse if, like Athena and Zeus, they stand high in their father's favor.

A predominant Hera tends to choose a strong mate, an alpha figure. She needs to feel secure, protected, and proud of him. When Zeus came to Hera as a small, helpless bird soaked from the rainstorm, he aroused her sympathy. However, it was when he revealed himself as the leader of the gods that she was willing to give herself to him, providing he sealed their union formally.

The fullest expression of the Hera archetype lies in her ability to be loyal and stand beside her partner no matter what happens. Her devotion is absolute and her love is unwavering. Hera's capacity for commitment is such that she deserves the respect and consideration that she yearns for.

In Your Natal Chart

The position of Juno in the natal chart reveals our attitudes toward and experiences of committed relationships. When Juno is a strong influence in the chart there is a desire or even a powerful need to seek a serious long-term partner. The astrological sign Juno is situated in is an indicator of the type of partner the person will find attractive and also shows the person's mode of expression within that relationship. The house in which Juno finds itself denotes how that need for union will be channeled.

If Juno's voice is quiet among the archetypes in the natal chart, it is more likely that this urge toward relationship will be channeled into other areas of life. Juno is a forceful character and is not generally attracted to people who are less powerful than herself. When there is no driving urge toward marital relationships, Juno's considerable energy can be directed instead toward business partnerships or friendships. The sexual aspect of union is less important to her than the feeling of trust and belonging.

When there are positive aspects, Juno's energy is experienced as tremendous loyalty, dedication, and devotion. Relationships are likely to be enduring because Juno ensures that the needs of both partners are met and because compromise is possible during rough patches. Challenging aspects to Juno can manifest as possessiveness and jealousy in which even siblings and friends can be viewed as a threat along with a strong competitive urge that has no compunction about knocking competitors out of the picture. Slights are taken to heart, and problems over issues of trust can be prominent.

Juno in the natal chart also gives clues about the attainment of a sense of fulfilment and the ability to express the nobler aspects of feminine nature. There is strong idealism present in this archetype that can be a force for good when properly channeled.

Rulership of Juno

Juno is most aptly suited to the rulership of Libra, the sign of partnership. The Libran urge to connect with another at a deep level is directed through Juno at a specific relationship that's carefully nurtured and fostered.

Of all the astrological signs, it is Libra who finds it most difficult to be alone. Librans need others for friendship and companionship, and the sense of isolation that can result if this is not forthcoming can make them feel depressed or physically ill. The Libran creativity and love of beauty are both aspects shared with Juno. Her beauty and the need for others to see and appreciate it reveal that she has more in common with Aphrodite/Venus than initially meets the eye. But where Aphrodite can be flighty and promiscuous, driven by the desire to merge fully with another in order to experience the alchemy of union, her attention tends to stray once the first flush of romance has faded. Juno, in contrast, brings constancy and desire for the security of an enduring relationship.

One of Juno's symbols is peacock feathers. Their iridescent colors and the eye in the center symbolize the goddess's pride and watchfulness. Little escapes her notice, and she rages against what she views as injustices. In Hera's story, it is the willingness of other women to be seduced by her husband that renders her incandescent with fury, to the extent of attempting to destroy those who sully the sanctity of marriage. Although the usually gentle Libran is less likely to wreak havoc, their sweet exterior will quickly disappear if they are faced with situations of injustice, and they will not hesitate to gird themselves and take action. "It's not fair" is a rallying call to Librans, and they are prepared to pour all of their energies into a cause that they consider to be worthy.

Juno and Librans prefer an ordered environment where the gaze can rest on beauty and harmony. Aesthetics are important to their well-being, and they are disturbed by disorder both internal and external because it interferes with the sense of peace they crave. This is also true of their appearance. Beautiful clothes, jewelry, and fragrances strengthen their sense of self, because both Juno and Librans need to feel accepted and admired by others.

Equality is a major issue in a relationship with their beloved, in friendships, and in the workplace. If Juno or Libra feel unappreciated, sparks can fly and, if the situation remains unchanged, they will retreat until a solution or compromise can be found. When their needs for equal consideration are met, harmony reigns and they are able to express their inner strength, poise, and charm.

Hera's darker element relate to the astrological sign Scorpio. The intensity of the Hera/Juno betrayal leads to extreme vengefulness as retaliation. To Scorpios, a loss of trust is initially devastating but then transforms into a cold fury capable of destroying everything in its path. Possessiveness is an aspect of the Scorpio nature, especially in relationships. The loved one must be theirs alone, a belief that can create power struggles and control issues. In the story of Zeus and Hera, Zeus was well aware of the effect his infidelities had on his wife, yet he was prepared to cause her agonizing emotional pain and put the lives of his lovers and their children at risk to prove to Hera that he could do as he pleased.

Because the marriage was stormy after the long honeymoon period came to an end, battles for control between Zeus and Hera were frequent. As leader of the gods, Zeus believed he deserved every privilege available. Hera was his equal, but Zeus was very much the alpha male. As the humiliated wife, Hera made bids to control her husband through harming the recipients of his sexual conquests. The Scorpionic refusal to give in and the impulse to battle to the death if necessary are strongly emphasized when there are strained aspects to Juno in the natal chart.

However, even the darker elements of Scorpio have the ability to achieve their redemption thanks to Juno's rulership. The attributes of willpower, tenacity, loyalty, and lasting attachment that cannot accept defeat are also borne out by Juno's affiliation with this astrological sign.

Chapter Fifteen

Pallas Athene— Athena

Athena/Pallas Athene rules Pallas Athene, Scorpio, and the eighth house.

Although a virgin goddess like Artemis and Hestia, Athena's temperament is very different from that of the wild Artemis and the gentle, spiritual Hestia. Early on, she swore to give her body to no man, and her sharp intellect and skill in battle make her equal to male gods and more than equal to mortal men. Born without a mother, she is powerful and independent, not given to displays of emotion, and commands loyalty and respect.

Athena's focus is on honing the mind and body to create a unified tool for clarity and effectiveness. Strong, wise, an adept strategist, she makes decisions based on careful consideration and refuses to act on impulse. Her self-sufficiency makes her formidable to those who are less capable. Her joy is in the perfect harmony of the body and mind as an instrument of the will.

The Birth of Athena

Athena's parents were Zeus and the titaness Metis, the daughter of Oceanus. Metis was renowned for her wisdom and herb lore, and it was she who prepared the emetic herbs that forced Kronos to regurgitate the children he had swallowed at birth after his defeat in a bid to prevent them from overthrowing him.

When Metis conceived, Zeus was warned by Gaia and Kronos that she would give birth to two children. The second, a boy, would take the throne of Zeus and rule in his stead. To avoid this, Zeus tricked Metis into becoming small, and then swallowed her. He averted the birth of a son by Metis that his parents predicted, but Athena grew within his forehead until the pain was so great that Zeus commanded Hephaestus to relieve the pressure by splitting open his forehead with an axe. Athena sprang out fully formed wearing golden armor and a helmet, carrying a spear. She became Zeus's favorite daughter, displaying the qualities of wisdom, intelligence, logic, and a cool head in battle to her father's great admiration.

Personality Traits

Athena was very much a man's woman; a trait that was extremely unusual and that earned her great respect among the male Olympians. She was beautiful and proud, courageous and level-headed, and she became an asset to Zeus and the only person he consulted about strategies. She was a mentor to many heroes and acted their protector and advisor.

Perseus was one who benefited from her support. When she discovered that Poseidon had seduced a woman named Medusa in one of her temples, she turned Medusa into a fearsome gorgon with snakes for hair and decided that Medusa must be slain. She advised Perseus to use his shield as a mirror so that he would not have to look upon her face, because to see the visage of Medusa would turn humans to stone. When Perseus confronted the gorgon, Athena guided his hand so that the sword he was wielding cut cleanly. She then took the head and mounted it upon her shield. Pegasus, the winged horse who sprang from Medusa's neck, was tamed with a golden bridle that Athena gave to another hero, Bellerophon, for that purpose.

When Heracles was driven insane by Hera and killed his wife and children, Athena aided him in carrying out the twelve labors he had to undertake in order to attain redemption.

The ten-year-long Trojan War that caused the death of many heroes, began when Paris, the son of King Priam of Troy, abducted the beautiful Helen, whom Aphrodite had gifted to him as the prize for choosing her as the loveliest of the goddesses. Through her anger at Paris, Athena sided with the Greeks and came to their aid repeatedly. Her favored hero was Achilles, the son of King Peleus of Thessaly and the sea nymph Thetis.

Poseidon and Zeus both desired Thetis and wished to have a child by her, but they were deterred from pursuing her when Prometheus warned them that her future son would be more powerful than his father. Instead, Zeus arranged for her to be married to a mortal, and Achilles was born soon after. Thetis dipped her child in the waters of the River Styx, which flowed through the underworld to make him immortal but held her son by his heel, which then became the only part of his body left unprotected.

Achilles learned the art of war from Chiron, his tutor and mentor. He was ferocious in battle, but even Athena could not save him when Paris discovered his vulnerable spot and shot an arrow into his heel, killing him.

Athena's sympathies were always with the men. When Orestes, the son of the hero Agamemnon and his wife Clytemnestra, killed his mother, Athena spoke up for him and insisted he be set free, arguing that Orestes had been justified in committing matricide. While Agamemnon had been away fighting in the Trojan war,

Clytemnestra had taken a lover. When her husband returned home ten years later, she and her lover murdered him. In despair and fury, Orestes slew his mother—the worst crime that could be committed in ancient Greece. It was only through Athena's intervention that his life was spared.

Athena was proud of her "male" attributes. She felt no hesitation about plunging into battle, and her admiration and friendship were reserved for men who were strong and courageous warriors and heroes. As daughter of the goddess of wisdom and the king of the gods, she inherited the most potent qualities of both parents and despised those who were emotional or foolhardy.

As a virgin goddess, Athena was insistent that no man could touch her. Her physical energy was channeled into warfare and her mental energy into the pursuit of knowledge. When Hephaestus attempted to rape her, Athena pushed him away. His semen fell to the ground and fertilized the earth. Gaia used her generative powers to birth a snake, Erichthonius, the serpent of wisdom, that Athena took to live with the Oracle and interpret the prophesies. A statue of Athena with a snake was later placed in the Acropolis in Athens to symbolize the attributes of wisdom and the power over life and death that she held.

Her rulership of Athens came about when the inhabitants of the city decided to choose a guardian deity. Both Athena and Poseidon put themselves forward, and each bestowed a gift to the citizens in order to influence their choice. Athena gave an olive tree and Poseidon gave a small spring. The Athenians chose Athena, and Poseidon vented his anger by flooding the plain that surrounded the city. The city was named after Athena and the olive tree became one of her emblems.

Athena's totem creature was the owl, a creature with a reputation for wisdom and knowledge as well as the ability to see in the dark and strike silently and instantly when prey appears.

Her competitive nature was aroused several times: once when Paris declared Aphrodite to be more beautiful than her, once when she and Poseidon vied for rulership of Athens, and again when her ambition to always be first and best among women was challenged by a mortal.

Athena and Arachne

One of Athena's domains was craftwork due to the skills needed in the creation of artefacts of beauty and intricacy, and her skill in weaving was a source of pride. Her ordered way of thinking and ability to see the completed article in her mind's eye coupled with the ability to hold that image until it was transferred through her nimble fingers made her a master weaver.

There are two versions to the story of Athena and Arachne. In one, Arachne's fame as a gifted weaver grew until other mortals were comparing her skill to that of Athena. In her fury, Athena turned her into a spider, serving as the origin of the word "arachnid."

In the second story, Arachne went to Athena and challenged her to a weaving competition. They each created a tapestry of great beauty, and Athena was impressed until she realized that the subject of Arachne's tapestry was Zeus in several of his guises in the act of seducing his paramours. Athena, closer to her father than to any other, was offended, insulted, and enraged. She destroyed the tapestry, and Arachne hanged herself. But before the mortal woman could die, Athena changed her into a spider that hung by a silken thread and devoted its life to spinning webs of great beauty and intricacy.

Relationships

Athena was a virgin goddess in the fullest expression of the term. She was self-contained, needing no one to be fulfilled and experience a sense of completeness within herself, and she was chaste. Unlike many of the other goddesses who were at the mercy of their emotions, Athena was cool and detached, ruled by her head instead of her heart.

Athena preferred the company of men, feeling comfortable, accepted, and respected for her understanding of warfare and keen intelligence. She had no desire for a consort, and her sensual energies were instead diverted into intellectual and creative pursuits. She derived pleasure from being viewed as and treated as an equal. Because of this, she was the least vulnerable of the goddesses. When slighted, her retaliation was swift and merciless, but when her support was given, she was always willing to do all that she could to help those whom she favored.

Athena's clear head made her a good strategist, and she was instrumental in giving advice and guidance to many heroes, who revered her and were intensely loyal to her.

Born from her father's forehead, active in the world of male gods and mortals, Athena appeared to have no thoughts of her mother, whom Zeus had imprisoned within him. She was disinterested in the traditional womanly pursuits, wiles, and grievances that she observed around her and was determined to remain true to herself.

Sibling Rivalry

Athena had a detached attitude toward her family with the exception of her father. Hera was deeply jealous of Athena's relationship with Zeus, particularly as Zeus had birthed Athena parthenogenically. Hera's ill-fated birthing of Hephaestus led to her rejection of him because he, with his club foot, could not compete with the beautiful and powerful warrior goddess. Later, Hephaestus attempted to force himself on her, but the snake born from his seed as it fell to the ground strongly embodied Athena's symbolic aspects, resulting in her adopting the serpent as her child. Athena's distrust in emotional matters meant that when it was strategic for her and her step-mother Hera to join forces temporarily against Zeus, it was accomplished without any unnecessary hard feelings on either side.

Her relationship with Ares was strained. He was envious of her position as their father's joint favorite (with Apollo), and Athena scorned his hot temper and inability to stay calm in battle. She also despised Ares for taking the side of the Trojans in the war and enlisted Zeus's permission to fight against Ares, ensuring that he was wounded.

Archetypal Resonance

Athena as an archetype embodies the qualities of intelligence, creative thinking, strategy-making, and emotional detachment. Her position as a woman among men in which she displayed the attributes of logical thinking, strategy, and the courage and determination to fight for her convictions makes her a powerful archetypal force.

Within the psyche, she is the voice of reason: strong, ambitious, undeterred by others' opinions unless they're considered be worthy of respect. She is the epitome of cool, clear logic that is able to see straight to the heart of a matter, refusing to be distracted from the task at hand.

This archetype steers clear of messy emotions that interfere with the powers of reasoning. If relationships are entered into, they are viewed more as a contract in which each person has agreed to its terms rather than through a rosy vision of romantic love, here considered both distasteful and foolish. If the contract is broken, the relationship is terminated.

Sexual impulses are often sublimated and diverted into channels that create mental rather than physical involvement, though these can also be viewed as a useful commodity. A love of knowledge opens the doors to serious academic study. An attunement to beauty and symmetry makes creative outlets that require planning and skill very appealing.

The Athena archetype is a gifted negotiator, mediator, and diplomat through her clear-sightedness and ability to examine a situation so that the most logical, workable course of action is clear. She earns respect from others, although she can be emotionally distant. Athena's golden armor represents the tendency of this archetype to guard against showing any form of weakness, which is anathema to her. There is a need to be viewed as strong and self-sufficient with no flaws visible that could make her vulnerable. Her armor protects her on two levels: it gives her privacy and security just as it allows her to avoid intimacy and keep her sense of autonomy. The gold of her armor also reflects the radiance of her mental faculties and insights.

Athena's driving motivation is the need to maintain independence and be valued for her intellectual and perceptual gifts, and respect for these qualities in those around her serves as her point of connection with others.

In Your Natal Chart

The name "Pallas Athene" stems from pre-Olympian times, when the Triple Goddess who contained within her the combination of maiden, mother, and crone was known in Libya as Pallas, Athene, and Medusa. Pallas was the virginal maiden, pure and clear-sighted. Athene was the mother of creative intelligence that manifested as fecundity, and Medusa was the crone in her guise as the death-dealing devourer of men. These three aspects became merged in ancient Greece, and Athena incorporated them as the wise, intelligent goddess who was also a fearsome opponent. She was later known to the Romans as Minerva.

In the natal chart, Pallas Athene's position reveals how we use our intelligence and powers of logical thinking. Pallas Athene brings a hunger for knowledge, clear perception, and talents in devising and following through plans and strategies to a person's natal chart. When this archetype is strong and positively aspected, there is tremendous insight, perception, planning power, strength, courage, and independence. A need for physical as well as mental activity is prevalent that can result in a love of sports, particularly competitive ones. Mental interests encompass a wide range to include any faculty that provides knowledge and adds to understanding. Strategic games such as chess are also popular with this archetype.

Challenging aspects to this asteroid can manifest as frustrating mental blocks, a conviction that others must always be in the wrong, and a refusal to listen to reason. When negatively aspected, Pallas Athene's independent nature can lead to a harsh determination to win at any cost where the end justifies the means. Conversely, some negative aspects can drain the self-confidence that provides the foundation for independence and can contribute toward a secretive, introverted personality more interested in books or computers than in people.

Pallas Athene's role as protector of and mentor to heroes is reflected in the natal chart as a strong sense of justice that, as with Hera/Juno, is very much on the side of who or what is right. If justice is not done, this archetype goes into battle with armor shining and weapons aimed with unerring accuracy. The force of will is such that any battles fought are rarely lost due to Pallas Athene's ability to plan out the most effective tactics in advance.

The astrological sign Pallas Athene is situated in denotes the manner through which Athena's influence is felt in the natal chart and in the psyche. In Taurus, for instance, her creative and intellectual faculties are channeled into creating works of beauty that appeal to the senses that which also have an intellectual or symbolic meaning. In Libra, she can manifest as a mediator and diplomat who is skilled at negotiating and sprinkles her elegant speech with words and phrases that are calculated to make an impact without causing offense.

Pallas Athene in the houses shows the areas of life in which intellect, independence, self-confidence, and determination will be channeled.

Rulership of Pallas Athene

Pallas Athene is most at home in Scorpio, the sign of indomitable will. The penetrating Scorpio mind is able to work well with Pallas Athene's gift of perceptiveness and ability to formulate strategies that take all sides of a situation into account. Scorpios tend to be excellent strategists due to their ability to hide their thoughts from others while being aware of undercurrents, just as they can plot an accurate course to their goal by observing which influences are around and making allowances for these. Like Pallas Athene, Scorpios dislike the thought of making mistakes and take care to ensure everything is under control.

Scorpio's domain is the art of war, where Pallas Athene has a lot of natural talent. Mars will rush in recklessly, following impulses and becoming caught in the heat of battle to the extent of losing his head. Scorpio, like Pallas Athene, has the inner drive and the passion for winning but is able to be patient and plot the course that will be most effective and ultimately lead more swiftly and surely to victory. Like Pallas Athene, Scorpios refuse to show signs of weakness. Their armor is strong and once a course is set, nothing can deter them from following through. Respect for others whose strength is equal to theirs predominates, as does the willingness to advise and protect those who are prepared to put effort in helping themselves. As enemies, they are merciless and will stop at nothing. Athena's determination to have Perseus slay Medusa for desecrating her sacred space is a heightened demonstration of the lengths to which Scorpionic nature is prepared to go in order to exact revenge.

Although Scorpio is considered the most sexual of the astrological signs, this energy can also be found in the kundalini, an element in the body's subtle energy system. Scorpio rules the base chakra, where kundalini energy is seated. The symbol for this energy is two snakes that entwine up the spine as they awaken and uncoil, representing the transformation of sexual energy into spiritual illumination. The Scorpio's ability to use this as a means of channeling the physical urges into a clear perception of a mentally and spiritually awakened state resonates strongly with Pallas Athene's totem of the snake.

Chapter Sixteen

Vesta — Hestia

Hestia/Vesta rules Vesta, Virgo, Scorpio, and the sixth and eighth houses.

Hestia is an embodiment of the virgin goddess along with Artemis and Athena. Hers is the realm of spirit; not the numinous, intangible realm of Poseidon/Neptune but the glow of the inner flame that lies at the center of the self and lights the way homeward.

The most retiring of the Olympians, Hestia prefers to exist in all homes and hearts rather than reside only with the gods beyond the reach of mortals. The flame that represents her is the flame of life itself that can be transferred from heart to heart, hearth to hearth. Hestia embodies the sanctuary both within the self and in the home and temple, where the self finds physical and spiritual sustenance.

The Birth of Hestia

Hestia was the oldest of the Olympian siblings. Born first and swallowed by Kronos, she was the last to leave his body when he regurgitated his children. Of all the family, she was the only one to retreat from Olympus voluntarily for more than brief periods of recuperation, and she chose instead to exist in a spiritual rather than humanized form. She was greatly revered and worshiped as the guardian of the hearth and the keeper of the sacred flame of life.

The quietest and most passive among the Olympians, Hestia remained in the background beyond the confines of the rowdy family circle yet was present as a unifying force. The symbolism of her sacred flame endures to the present: the Olympic torch is lit from Hestia's flame to mark the beginning of the Olympic Games, a celebration of the body's strength and endurance as well as the power of spirit that fuels the physical form.

The Hearth

The goddess elected to be portrayed as a flame rather than take a physical form. Her nature was the homeland of warmth, inspiration, nourishment, and comfort, and the circular hearths and temples built in her honor represented the unbroken circle of life and the wholeness encompassed within it. Hestia chose to live within the home and heart of every deity and mortal.

The hearth was the central focus of the home, where families could gather together and be warmed by the fire and in each other's company. As the fire was also used for cooking food, it was the source of nourishment. Gazing into the flames could elicit visions and meditative states, opening the mind to the silent spaces within where spiritual insights could be accessed. Hestia's flame burned within every home, creating a connection between each member of the family with the wider community. The first flame in a newly built hearth was ceremonially carried there from its source, the mother-fire, so that the goddess's essence spread to encompass all.

In each home was an altar to Hestia where she received the choicest offerings of all deities yet offended none of her siblings, who also revered her. Felt through the warmth of the fire, her physical and spiritual presence was a constant reminder of her guardianship.

The Temple

In pre-Olympian times, the Goddess was worshiped in an earthier manner than during and after the rise of the Olympians. The followers of the Great Goddess in her triple aspect of maiden, mother, and crone were guided by priestesses who tended the sacred flame of life. Although considered to be virgins in the sense of being independent and autonomous, they were also sexually active in the service of the Great Goddess. The men who came to learn more about the nature of the Goddess were taught by her followers to respect the sexual and spiritual union of the god and goddess within. Children born from these rites were considered gifts from the Goddess.

With the coming of the Olympians, Hestia embodied the connection with the soul and the eternal flame that burns within. The sacred marriage of the union of the god and goddess aspects took place within the self, integrating the anima and animus within the psyche and opening the perception to a knowledge of the spiritual realms through devotional practices and a simplicity of lifestyle.

Hestia and her Roman counterpart, Vesta, vowed to remain virgins and refused all offers of marriage. The Romans built a circular temple to Vesta where her maidens, the vestal virgins, lived and worshiped. These maidens were chosen at a young age (usually around six) and were contracted to remain at the temple in the service of Vesta for thirty years. After that time they could leave, though most of them chose to stay. The rules for living in the temple were strict: the sacred flame had to be continually tended and never allowed to go out; chastity, devotion, and humility were essential. If rules were broken, the punishment was harsh—a vestal virgin who lost her virginity was condemned to a slow death, buried alive underground. However, Vesta's maidens held privileges not bestowed on other women. They were autonomous, independent from men, free of society's patriarchal rules, and revered beyond the confines of the temple. Vestal virgins were given charge of contracts and important documents, as their purity and respect for the privacy of others made them supremely trustworthy.

Personality Traits

Hestia was gentle and quiet. She chose not to live on Olympus; instead, the hearth and fire were her living embodiments. As a virgin goddess she was self-contained and complete, having no need of any outer influence to cultivate her sense of self. Whereas the other virgin goddesses, Artemis and Athena, chose companions (for Artemis her nymphs and Athena her heroes and warriors), Hestia preferred solitude. Although her vestal virgins lived in the temple dedicated to her and kept her eternal flame alive, Hestia's presence was felt by all people, everywhere through the hearth fire. She asked for no offerings or special treatment other than that her fire was kept burning and was the best-loved of the goddesses. Her calm poise and connection with the spiritual nature shared by all were traits that others sought to emulate. Her focus was on the total absorption with the spiritual self that made any task, however mundane or dreary, an act of devotion and dedication.

Her detachment held nothing of Athena's coolness. Hestia's detachment was instead fostered in the understanding that life's dramas and longings were essentially born from a yearning for unity with a force greater than the small, limited self. Because of this, every action took on an aspect of sacredness that created a sense of harmony and connection with the life-force. Her loving nature was apparent each time a fire warmed the surrounding air.

Hestia was set apart from the relationships between the other gods and goddesses. She had no interest in petty jealousies or conquests. Instead, she preferred solitude, with its wide-open spaces within the mind, where thoughts could soar to touch the Infinite. Unlike her siblings, she was unconcerned about external appearances or others' opinions of her. Her sense of peace and completeness set her apart and allowed her to observe all from a state of tolerant compassion.

Relationships

Hestia rejected all advances made to her. Her sexual impulses were channeled into her inner self, and the calmness and purity she radiated gave her an aura of quiet confidence. Artemis and Athena's active nature found expression in hunting and warfare. In Hestia, it was directed into meditation and contemplation.

Poseidon and Apollo, brother and nephew respectively, both wished to marry her. Hestia declined their offers and gently asserted her wish to remain chaste and pure. She was no doubt an attractive prospective wife for both powerful gods; the embodiment of the still, calm center for the stormy-natured sea god and a haven of peace and tranquility for the god of the sun who needed his yearly retreat to Hyperborea to recharge. Instead, Zeus agreed to allow Hestia to remain virginal and gave her the gift of a place within every home's hearth.

Sibling Rivalry

Although secluded and independent, Hestia was closely associated with Hermes through their guardianship of the home. Whereas Hestia's sacred place was the hearth and fire, Hermes was the protector of the threshold, the border between outside and inside. These two deities ensured that the home was a place of safety and security. The old marriage custom in which the husband carries his new wife over the threshold of their new home is in honor of Hermes. In ancient times, an altar would be set up near the hearth where both deities could be honored.

Archetypal Resonance

Hestia as an archetype embodies the search for meaning and fostering simplicity in life. She is the quiet, calm voice in the psyche that needs to be carefully listened to in order to be heard among the other archetypes' more assertive voices. A need for time alone, an urge toward approaching life spiritually, a love of silence, and a perception of holiness (inner wholeness) in every task are all attributes related to her.

This self-contained goddess steps to the fore whenever there is the wish to allow the world to drift by as you sit and watch in peace, uninvolved in the noise, activity, and drama. Fastidiousness is one of her qualities because the body and mind are equally respected, and the body is considered a temple of the soul. "Soul" itself is a word that resonates closely with Hestia as the life force underpinning every activity, no matter how menial or significant. When things are done soulfully, we experience it as a continual expression of our light from our inner world as it radiates to the outer world.

In Your Natal Chart

Vesta's position in your natal chart reveals how and where you seek out inner stillness and silence. The brightest of the asteroids, it shines its light through the sign and house in which it is situated, gently encouraging us to express a commitment to a lightness of being that is detached from worldly cares and considerations. The sacred fire that Vesta embodies is the flame of inner warmth and nurturing, accompanied by a strong yet peaceful sense of self.

When combined with aspects to other planets, this flame can be fanned by the breath of sensuality and sexuality that considers sex a sacred act of pure love and devotion. The ancient role of Hestia/Vesta as an embodiment of the Great Goddess still lives within us and can be awoken if the right person appears—one who has an attitude toward relationship as the joining of the inner as well as outer male and female.

Without aspects between planets to act as the prince to the Sleeping Beauty of Vesta's purity, the asteroid brings a focus to the sign and house it is found in that allows independent thought and action, compassion without attachment, and profound thought processes and insight.

If there are challenging aspects to Vesta, it can manifest as either a fear of solitude due to reluctance to delve too deeply into the meaning and purpose of life's challenges, or conversely, there can be an aloofness that creates a personality cut off from others and the source of the life-force. Issues around sexuality can also be prominent in difficult aspects to Vesta that can take the form of frigidity, promiscuity, or confused relationships because the sense of self is weakened and therefore vulnerable or undefined. Depending on which planets and aspects are involved, the boundaries that Vesta maintains can either be ineffective or are built so high that they imprison the self.

When strong and well-aspected in the natal chart, Vesta helps to define a clear-cut sense of self and purpose as well as a keen, enquiring mind that seeks to illuminate itself. There is a propensity for hard work because work is viewed as sacred service. In that expression is the ability to connect with the sacred and spiritual in all areas of life as well as a warm, calm demeanor. Love is easily inspired because there is a soft glow that emanates from the core of being that elicits a welcoming warmth from others in return.

Rulership of Vesta

Vesta is the ruler of both Virgo and Scorpio, and the connection with Virgo is easily apparent. The pictorial symbol for this sign is the virgin carrying a sheaf of grain, denoting connections within the Virgoan nature with both Vesta and Ceres/Demeter. In its rulership of Virgo, Vesta accentuates the qualities of purity, chasteness, clarity of thought, dedication, devotion to others through service, and detached aloofness. The calm Virgoan exterior hides an active inner life, and through Vesta the realms of the spirit are accessed.

Unless strongly aspected, the Virgoan attitude toward relationships has a noticeable affinity with Vesta. Virgoans are more likely to be content to be alone and single than any other sign in the zodiac, and they highly value their independence and autonomy. Their love of cleanliness and order makes them good housekeepers and homemakers, but the main motivation for the maintenance of tidiness, harmony, and cleanliness is that an uncluttered environment helps to keep the mind clear.

Virgo's perfectionism is reflected in Vesta's insistence upon truth and order as well as a clear code for living based on honesty and integrity.

The connection with the sacred space that is the home is found in Mercury and Vesta. As the pillar that guards the threshold, Mercury provides a source of masculine strength and independence. As the circular hearth within, Vesta provides a feminine source of warmth and light. Part of Virgo's self-sufficiency is the inner recognition of both god and goddess within.

Vesta's rulership of Scorpio is less immediately apparent until we remember this luminous goddess's pre-Olympic role. The rites to the Great Goddess were performed between the priestesses and men who came to them to honor the goddess in both her physical and spiritual form. The sexual acts that took place were transcendental, transforming the climax of each participant into a spiritual charge that elevated them to the temporary status of god and goddess. The union was viewed as complete within itself, and relationships were not forged between the priestesses and men other than during the single experience of the act of transformation. Children born from this were considered sacred. The sexual act was, in essence, a contract between man and priestess to strive for the highest spiritual state: a circumstance that exists to the present day in the Ayurvedic practice of tantra, the art of ecstasy that leads to enlightenment.

Vesta's rulership of Scorpio highlights the attitude toward physical pleasures. Vesta's high ideals and extreme selectiveness coupled with a strong sense of self that makes it difficult to surrender fully to another person makes this combination of sign and asteroid discriminating when selecting a partner. Vesta is a perfectionist and, so is Scorpio in its own way.

Vesta's rulership makes the Scorpionic intensity of thought and need to discover causes and hidden meanings profound. Scorpio's urge toward transformation and renewal finds symbolism in the inner flame that Vesta embodies. Just as the phoenix, a Scorpionic totem, hurls itself into the fire only to be reborn, so does Scorpio eagerly enter the flames of transformation to allow the old, limited self to die and then re-emerge more potent and powerful from the renewed connection with the sacred.

Chapter Seventeen

Relationships and Aspects

Understanding the relationships between the deities whose myths underpin the planets' symbolism can make the interpretation of the astrological aspects much easier and clearer.

Aspects are the mathematical relationships between the planets that demonstrate an effect on the mode of expression of each planet involved. Some aspects are beneficial, others create tension, but all create a point of connection vital to understanding the natal chart and its dynamics. In this chapter you will find examples of how you can interpret the aspects through their archetypal resonance as well as in the traditional manner.

An easy way to work out the dynamics of the deities through the aspects is to imagine that you are having a party and that each archetype is one of your guests. If Venus and Mars are in conjunction (very close to each other), the sexual sparks that fly between them could add an interesting charge to the atmosphere, because Aphrodite and Ares were lovers. Conversations between other guests might be less noticeable than the dialogue taking place between Venus and Mars. Their energy could bring added vitality and spark to the party, or it could leave some of the more chastely-aspected guests feeling rather embarrassed. Pallas Athene might find the situation irritating and irrelevant and try to bring some culture to the floor show. Vesta may quietly withdraw unless other connections are present through her aspects that bring Hestia's earthier, pre-Olympian role to the fore.

Now, as all of the guests are elements of yourself, the dynamics are taking place within your psyche, and the choices as to whether you decide to ignore what's going on between Venus and Mars or enjoy it, get involved in an intellectual conversation with Pallas Athene, catch up on gossip with Mercury, or discuss children with Demeter is entirely up to you. The connections between the archetypes and how you respond to their influences are revealed through your natal chart, but expression of these archetypes in your life can be understood and worked with so that they ultimately become more beneficial for you.

The Conjunction

A conjunction occurs when two planets sit side by side in the natal chart. Its orb (sphere of influence) is between 0 and 8 degrees either side. Often positive, its effect can be detrimental depending on the planets involved, as this aspect brings added strength to (or can sap the strength of) both planets in the relationship.

Example

A conjunction between the Sun and the Moon brings together Apollo and Artemis, the twin children of Zeus and Leto. It can create tension, as their individual modes of expression are very different.

The willpower and competitive nature between these siblings can cause a clash similar to what occurred between Apollo and

Artemis when he duped her into killing Orion, her lover. The retiring nature of the Moon rejects the Sun's forcefulness, resulting in a temporary loss of strength. A Sun-Moon conjunction is most powerful when aspects are also made to other planets in the natal chart. If Mars is connected to either planet, the active aggressive principle is activated, bringing dominance to the aspected planet. If Mars is linked to the Moon, Artemis will subvert Apollo's willpower. If Mars is linked to the Sun, emotions and intuition will be ignored and the logical mind will dominate.

When the Sun is conjunct Mercury in the natal chart, the brothers Apollo and Hermes (Mercury) stand side by side. They need a certain distance in their relationship, as it began in the wrong footing in the Greek myths, with Hermes stealing Apollo's prized cattle. Their differences were resolved and a truce was called, but only after Hermes gave his lyre to Apollo.

The astrological interpretation of a conjunction between the Sun and Mercury depends on how close the planets are to each other. If they are joined at the hip, so to speak, with an orb of less than 4 degrees, it creates what is called a combust conjunction. In this type of situation, both planets are combustible—they burn each other out. Imagine it as a fight between the two brothers from which both emerge bruised and exhausted, no power left for their individual traits to be effective. The astrological effect is an over-abundance of solar energy that fries the brain and makes the thought processes confused. Neither side can express their true nature effectively.

If there is a safer distance between Apollo and Mercury, an orb of between 4 and 8 degrees, they can get on very well. The Sun's creativity and urge for self-expression can spark Mercury's intellectual capabilities and communication skills to bring an abundance of brilliant, workable ideas that heightens positivity, friendliness, and eloquence to the personality, making them popular with others.

The Sextile

A distance of 60 degrees between planets with a 5-degree orb on either side is called a sextile. This is a harmonious aspect that brings about friendly relationships.

Example

A sextile between Venus and Saturn brings interesting possibilities. Kronos, Saturn's deity, symbolizes the need to work with limitations and impose discipline. In the Greek myths, he swallowed his children in order to hold onto his power. He was then taken up by the Romans and became their fatherly, fertile god of agriculture and of time. Venus is free-flowing, a creative, sexual, and social butterfly. The pair would not make a good match at first glance, but in this aspect they do.

Venus embodies beauty, harmony, and artistic gifts. Saturn embodies restraint and boundaries. A sextile between these two planets is often found in the charts of talented artists, where Saturn gives the self-discipline and use of time that enables beautiful ideas to take form and find their expression. The gift of creativity needs this in order to bring shape to ideas.

The Square

When there is a distance of 90 degrees between two planets within an orb of 8 degrees on either side, it is called a square and is an indication of challenges that must be addressed. These can either overwhelm you or be used as a springboard for achievement. Often it is the challenges that we face that test our mettle; our determination to overcome these can bring a personality added strength.

Example

The relationship between Zeus and Ares in Greek myths was very strained, and it plays out if there is a square aspect between Jupiter and Mars, their astrological counterparts. Zeus despised Ares because of his inability to employ logic. The rashness and impetuousness of his son's nature irritated him in the extreme. In turn, Ares's rejection by his father only served to make him more rebellious and determined to go his own way. Their relationship was one of intense dislike and conflict.

A square aspect between Jupiter and Mars echoes this situation within the psyche. The Jovian expansiveness and power are diverted into aggression and a destructive attitude that leads to extremes in behavior. Jupiter's benevolence becomes twisted into a desire for self-aggrandizement, and the approach to others can be harsh and dictatorial.

However, a positive aspect such as a sextile can ease the strain between the two archetypes. Mars's energy and drive can instead be put to use by Jupiter's optimism and urge toward growth and expansion. The difficult relationship between father and son can be healed, as each discovers that the other has qualities that are valuable and constructive.

The Trine

A trine forms when there is a distance of 120 degrees between two planets with an 8-degree orb either side. It's a beneficial aspect that brings out the very best in the archetypes linked in it.

Example

A trine between Jupiter and Ouranos brings together the highest qualities of both deities and planets. In the myths, Ouranos was the grandfather of Zeus (Jupiter). His reign was terminated when his son Kronos overthrew and emasculated him, leaving him to retreat into the background. But as the first sky god whose generative power was contained within the forces of thunder and lightning, he bequeathed his thunderbolt to Zeus, who only used it as a weapon when absolutely necessary. The beneficial interaction between these two deities and planets brings the powers of thunder and lightning to the fore in the form of intense sparks and flashes of creative insight.

Jupiter's expansive nature is then able to increase Ouranos's electromagnetic properties, manifesting as true leadership qualities and the ability to perceive solutions to problems not apparent to others around them. The combined energy of these two powerful sky gods brings depth and profundity of thought and even flashes of genius that can create long-lasting individual and collective change.

The Opposition

An opposition is found in the natal chart when two planets are placed directly opposite each other at 180 degrees apart with an orb of 8 degrees either side. Oppositions create tension, rather like two people facing each other in an argument, though occasionally the saying that opposites attract can be true in astrology. Dialogue and intervention are necessary for balance to be achieved, and other aspects to one or both planets concerned (such as sextiles and trines) can help defuse the potential for internal psychological conflict.

Example

If Ceres and Pluto are in opposition in the natal chart, it can bring about an internal scenario similar to the mythological situation between Demeter and Hades. In the story, Hades abducted Persephone, Demeter's beloved daughter, carrying her off to the underworld to be his wife. Demeter's grief was such that she froze over the earth until her daughter was returned to her. Yet even after Persephone's return, she had to share her time between Hades and Demeter due to entering a contract to her husband before leaving his realm.

An opposition between Ceres and Pluto indicates power struggles in life that come about in attempts to hold on too tightly to that which is dear to you. The fear of loss is so great that the creative urges can be used destructively; the opposition's challenge challenge is to learn to let go and compromise.

Soul Patterns

Holding the stories of the myths in mind can help you understand the dynamics prevalent between planetary and asteroid positions and aspects in your natal chart. Each planet and asteroid represent an element within the psyche, and the archetypal patterns that emerge from their relationships can enable you to discover resolutions to difficulties that allow for new strength and growth. However, the aspects have even more to tell you.

When the natal chart is created and lines are drawn between the planets, a pattern emerges. This pattern forms a picture, a mirror of the soul that enables you to see an image of what motivates you to discover and carry out your purpose in life.

The natal chart is a map of the heavens at the moment of your birth as you would see it if you could look up at the sky as a newborn child. The birth chart is the key to your personality and potential, and it can be used to unlock the inner self's secrets. The pattern among your aspects can help—its shapes can be read intuitively. For example, you may see combinations of lines that seem to form a flower, a butterfly, a pyramid, or a boat. Allow your imagination to fly free when you look at your aspects' pattern, and it will reveal much of your soul life. The spark of recognition it engenders can have a transformative effect on how you view yourself.

Astrology is a complex science, and there are many good books that can help you interpret your natal chart step by step through the planets in the signs and houses as well as the aspects. After that is cultivating the ability to integrate the information. As the purpose of this book is exploring the connection between the myths and the planets, an in-depth interpretation of all of factors that can be taken into account in the natal chart is not included. But the stories of the deities can open you up to a fresh perspective on the journey, the discovery that fuels the study of astrology. Through their resonances with the planets and asteroids, the ancient myths that still live on within the psyche enable us to better understand ourselves and others.

Conclusion

Harmonizing the Voices

Through undertaking this journey through the archetypes and planets as well as applying your understanding of both, you may have discovered that this is just the beginning of a greater journey toward helping yourself and others to fulfil your extraordinary potential. The power of our mind and our imagining is infinite. Within the mind are the seeds for all that we could become. Also within our mind is the negator of that potential, the swallower of the creative children of our imagination. The choices we make about whether to allow ourselves to fulfil our potential are based on how much attention we pay, if any, to the inner self and its voices that whisper in our psyche.

As they sing through the clashing or harmonizing chords in the mind, the archetypes are brought to light and life through their planetary counterparts in our natal chart. Some make their voices heard more than others, but they are all present, offering their gifts and their challenges, arguing amongst themselves, making love, making war, creating harmony or discord. If we accept and honor them, we learn to accept and honor ourselves. If we work with them, they can lend us the clarity, strength, and power to fulfil our purpose in being here. But first we need to reach for the volume controls.

When the noisier archetypes are allowed to have their way, it can be at the expense of the quieter ones. If you are in a room where one or two people are shouting above the music, the music itself appears to become discordant. When this happens in the natal chart, we can turn down the volume, adjust the bass and treble, and find more inner balance and harmony. To that end, the loudest voices may not be the archetypes you may expect from the myths; it may not be Mars, or Mercury, or Jupiter. It could be Pluto, keeping you in the underworld and cautioning you to wear your cap of invisibility as Hades did. It could be Vesta telling you that relationships are not necessary, or Ceres saying that all that matters is the role as parent. What is important is to find balance and use your gifts wisely and well.

The natal chart reveals strengths and weaknesses. We can employ our understanding of archetypes to turn down the volume of the ones taking control and find ways to allow them to be better integrated with the others. We can also play up strengths and learn to develop them. If the planetary configuration has elements of inner conflict that hold you back, you can reduce it by observing what elements harmonize with them and obtain their help. If Mars and Jupiter are squaring up (seemingly preparing for psychological conflict), you can enlist the help of Venus with her loving nature or Pallas Athene with her logic and mediation skills. Vesta may be called upon to allow a quiet inner space where resolution can be found, or you could call to Mercury, who can encourage inner dialogue between the warring elements and act as a guide through to the light of release and joy. We are never entitled to use our natal chart as an excuse for not resolving inner challenges. Obstacles are present so that we can learn to negotiate them and grow stronger through that process.

Often the quietest voices in the psyche are the ones offering the most wisdom; the loudest are frequently the ones clamoring for our attention because they crave harmony. By looking at who is seated where in the mind's pantheon and listening to what they have to say, we can find ways that allow them to be heard more clearly and thus open ourselves up to increased inner harmony and unity.

I hope that you've found this book useful, and I wish for you all that you wish for yourself.

With love and blessings,
Lisa

Recommended Reading

Albert, Liv. *Greek Mythology: The Gods, Goddesses and Heroes Handbook*. Adams Media, 2001.

Apollodorus and Robin Hard. *The Library of Greek Mythology*. Oxford University Press, 2008.

Bolen, Jean Shinoda. *Goddesses in Everywoman: Powerful Archetypes in Women's Lives*. Harper, 2014.

Bolen, Jean Shinoda. *Gods in Everyman: Archetypes That Shape Men's Lives*. Harper, 2014.

Buxton, Richard. *The Complete World of Greek Mythology*. Thames and Hudson, 2004.

Camp, John, and Elizabeth Fisher. *Exploring the World of the Ancient Greeks*. Thames and Hudson, 2002.

Fry, Stephen. *Mythos: The Greek Myths Retold*. Chronicle Books, 2019.

George, Demetra, and Douglas Bloch. *Asteroid Goddesses: The Mythology, Psychology, and Astrology of the Re-Emerging Feminine*. Nicolas-Hays, Inc., 2003.

Giesecke, Annette. *Classical Mythology A to Z: An Encyclopedia of Gods & Goddesses, Heroes & Heroines, Nymphs, Spirits, Monsters, and Places*. Black Dog and Leventhal, 2020.

Graves, Robert. *The Greek Myths*. Viking, 2018. Originally published 1955 by Penguin Books.

Hamilton, Edith. *Mythology: Timeless Tales of Gods and Heroes*. Back Bay Books, 2013. Originally published 1942 by Little, Brown & Co.

Hughes, Ted. *Tales from Ovid: 24 Passages from the Metamorphoses*. Faber & Faber, 1997.

Hallam, Elizabeth. *Gods and Goddesses: A Treasury of Deities and Tales from World Mythology*. Blanford, 1996.

Lefkowitz, Mary. *Greek Gods, Human Lives: What We Can Learn from Myths*. Yale University Press, 2003.

Matyszak, Philip. *The Greek and Roman Myths: A Guide to the Classical Stories*. Thames and Hudson, 2010.

Menzies, Jean. *Greek Myths: Gods and Goddesses*. Macmillan, 2023.

Russo, Lucas. *Uncovering Greek Mythology*. Self-published, 2021.